IN SEARCH OF
"CONGRUENCE"
- AND SUCCESS IN SELLING

Written by Kieran Maloney
In collaboration with Barrie Smith

In Search of "Congruence" - and Success in selling

First published in 2012 by

Ecademy Press
48 St Vincent Drive,
St Albans,
Hertfordshire,
AL1 5SJ

info@ecademy-press.com

www.ecademy-press.com

Printed and Bound by Lightning Source in the UK and USA

Set in Warnock Pro by Charlotte Mouncey

Printed on acid-free paper from managed forests.
This book is printed on demand, so no copies will be remaindered
or pulped.

ISBN 978-1-908746-30-6

Acknowledgements

Our gratitude and thanks go to all those colleagues and clients we have worked with over the years. Discussing and debating with them has constantly helped us move forward on this journey of discovery. We also thank those of you who will read this book and add to the debate as we know the journey is never ending and new ideas, understandings and concepts will always emerge.

Particularly Barrie's thanks go to:

Shaun Astley-Stone: For never letting business get in the way of friendship

Bill Douglas: For demonstrating that you cannot manage results, you _must_ manage activity.

Ian Dike: For the importance of asking open questions

Len Enoch: For a lifetime of inspiration and friendship

Clyde Lawrence: For his formula for managing stress: "Stop worrying about it and worry _at_ it".

Rob Saunders: For the loyalty and friendship of the most effective Sales Manager I have known

And Kieran's thanks go to:

Dr. Anat Bardi: For her patience and insights into the psychology of groups of people

Gene Barkatullah: For inspiration and being a great manager

Richard Davies: For insights and helping me think of Behaviours and characteristics

Barrie Smith: For friendship, insight into selling and being a great business partner

Dr. Michael Wolff: For taking a chance on me and having faith in me

Also to the hundreds, maybe thousands of sales professionals we have met in our careers.

Foreword

Is your company's future dependent on sales success? Are you involved in training or educating successful sales persons? Are you already a successful professional salesperson or are you considering a career in selling? Do you recognise that the market place today is increasingly presenting new challenges? Are you seeking to refresh your approach or indeed develop new skills to meet the demands of achieving sales success in this age when buyers are better informed than ever before? How easy is it to achieve success in today's challenging market place?

Like most things the art of selling is changing. Two contrasting developments set the scene for an emerging paradigm change in successful selling. First, a relatively new development is recognition that neither the rigid separation of the marketing and sales functions or the total integration of these functions is any longer valid. Once the essential product characteristics and promotional platform have been agreed, the sales process requires sales people with broader marketing understanding as well as selling know how. The second development is an old one that has recently been re discovered; the psychology involved in buying decisions is based on emotional and not rational decisions.

The global economy has created greater choice and opportunity. As we write we are in the midst of a deep economic downturn. The web gives customers the means to compare products and prices; competition has never been greater; information has never been so readily available.

This changed environment demands new levels of sales skills and yet never has there been a greater need for the professional sales person to have a bedrock of tried and tested capabilities. It is against this background that the professional sales person of today is as important as the product in presenting the customer with the essential Unique Selling Proposition.

We have argued for many years that, to be truly successful in a sales career, as a Manager or a Sale Maker, basic and fundamental Behaviours, Attitudes, Skills and Knowledge must be continuously critiqued, developed and polished to meet the progressive demands of each generation of customers. In the current generation sound bites, networks and personalised branding has turned selling upside down but many of the fundamentals for success remain and must be re-engineered to deliver the necessary confidence for successful selling.

Based on our successful sales improvement work shops we have identified in this book the key elements of a successful sales approach which must be broadened to understand the essential and little understood point of alignment between the sale maker and the customer. This is the 'Point of Congruence.' It is at this point that you will have achieved Success in Selling.

"In Search of Congruence - and Success in Selling" will take you through the following four eras of selling and highlight the development of the fundamental sales skills that lead us eventually to Congruence

- The Era of Consolidation, in which product integrity, values, belief systems and Beliefs, Attitudes, Skills and Knowledge are explained

- The Era of Expansion, in which customer choice and bargaining power, brand development, product cycles and selling response are identified

- The Era of Ambition, in which the Behaviours, Attitudes, Skills and Knowledge of the sales person are developed to accommodate the aggressive customer attitudes of "I Want and I Will Have"

- The Era of Realism, in which we see how customers have developed their own Buying Process and we introduce selling techniques to meet this challenge

We are ambitious enough to hope that this book will become the essential companion for successful salespersons. Reading the book, understanding its implications and adopting the principles will lead to improved sales success for *you*. It has for the many sales people who have attended our successful workshops.

It has been our privilege to help the careers of literally thousands of sales people in both the U.K. and countries from Africa, Asia, Australasia and the Americas.

In the coming years we hope this will continue and that you will gain Sales Success from your introduction to the ideas in this book.

Sincerely,

Kieran Maloney & Barrie Smith

Contents

In Search of "Congruence"
: an introduction

They say that a journey of a thousand miles starts with just one step. Most will tell you that you need a map, or a satellite navigation system and a destination in mind before you embark. The interesting thing about journeys is that things happen on the way that may take you to new, more exciting and better places.

The start of our journey and search was the question "So where does the customer feature in the sales process?" We weren't sure that "Congruence" was what we were searching for but that is what we discovered.

This question has brought us to where we are today, but we didn't know that this would be a destination.

We started our progression by analysing the process customers undertake whenever they make a purchase. The analysis revealed the map or navigation system that the customer uses to make a buying decision.

Further research confirmed that whatever the purchase the navigation remained the same – the buying process.

We then examined many formats and examples of sales processes and presentations. 'RANCS'[1], 'PISPRC[2]' or 'CiCaGrCoCl[3]'; the acronyms were many and complex.

Our experience suggested though that to be successful a sales process should match and enhance The Buying Process. When the potential buyer and the sales professional reach a point of "Congruence", the sale can be achieved.

---

1   RANCS: Relax, Ask questions, find Needs, gain Commitment Summarise

2   PISPRC: Preparation Introduction Stock check, Presentation Resale, Closure

3   CiCaGrCoCl: Create Interest, Command Attention Give Reasons, Conclude Clinch

The progression to "Congruence" immediately became the model for our work with the sales teams of our customers and led to the requests we received for writing this book.

As a professional sales person you will have several questions in mind as you open this book and debate why, how, what, when, and where this may be useful to you and, anyway who are the people who wrote it?

Well here are some answers to those questions for you.

Who are the people who have written this?

By way of introduction, I am Kieran Maloney. My background as a developer of people started out in formal education and has, for the past twenty-five years embraced the world of business and commerce where I have focused on the transference of learning and practical, pragmatic psychology. My collaborator Barrie Smith is a sales professional who has had a career in sales and sales management over a period of forty years. In that time he has had success in achieving many sales goals in a variety or markets and also in contributing to the training and development of hundreds of sales professionals.

In combining my experience and interest as a "people developer" with Barrie's Knowledge and understanding of selling, we believe we have, in this book, created something different and special. The drawing together of the experience of a successful salesman with the insight of pragmatic psychology makes this an unusual and different book.

With many years of sales experience in many different fields, Barrie has brought his learning together to provide practical guidance for sales people and formed a strategic approach that will appeal to sales managers and directors. Integrate this with the understanding of people and the practical and applied psychology which we provide and this book offers a very different perspective on selling.

In combining our experiences we hope to provide very real and practical guidance for sales people, regardless of their precise role. Although the situations may vary and the world is constantly changing, the earliest experiences and the lessons learned remain as vibrant and current today as they were when Barrie first encountered them.

We have worked together for many years now, combining our experience for the benefit of our clients, their sales teams, their customers and their shareholders. And so to answer questions you may have in mind:

Why have we written this book?

In short because we were asked to by many of the people we have helped in the past. Our passion over many years has been to develop professional salesmen. Our intention is to excite, enthuse, educate and empower sales professionals.

How should you use this book?

It is designed to give you exposure to contemporary ideas and approaches to successful selling based upon our experience and learning over many years of selling, educating and understanding people and what makes them "tick". There is reference to the environment and the eras through which our selling practice and knowledge have developed. Nothing is lost; all that we talk about is relevant today although it may have a slightly different focus from when we first learned it.

Enjoy the journey and take time to reflect on your own, every step of the way! If it suits you, why not read with a pencil in hand and make notes in here or in a separate note book.

So you can find what you are looking for, each chapter ends with a summary wherein you will find a synopsis of the key elements described in the chapter. Also at the end there is a listing of the key developments of selling showing the progression of each era so you may find any special areas or items that you are looking for.

What will you gain from reading this book?

We believe that every reader who aspires to become a sales professional or who already has sales experience will benefit from reading this book. For some readers it will be a reaffirmation of what you do well already, with perhaps some useful ideas and challenges that you can integrate into your sales approach. For other readers much more of it may be new.

For all our readers we believe it will provide an interesting historical perspective on where we are today and why selling is so important and at the same time explain some of the psychology behind what happens in the sales interaction.

Customers have changed and have greater access to information on products, services, pricing and competitor information. Selling in this environment demands a different approach, whether you are selling to a business or an individual consumer. Understanding how and what enables and encourages customers to buy adds to a competitive advantage and our experience shows that this approach is really successful. It adds satisfaction to the sales person's role and it adds to their success AND the bottom line profitability of a company.

The practical experiences explored in the four eras build to the latest approach explored at the end of the book. We suggest that all sales people may wish to read each chapter in turn and gain an insight into what works and WHY it works.

As I mentioned, Barrie and I have worked together in various guises for about fifteen years at the time this book was written. Constantly challenging each other and building upon our joint Knowledge and experiences, our approach to sales has remained alive and vital. The principles explained in this book ARE successful and if applied with rigour and confidence they yield results. For some of our readers this appears to be a radically different approach, for others it is a logical extension of existing practice and some may already be adopting these principles without fully understanding how and why they work.

When does this book become useful?

From the moment you open it. We started this introduction with the six open questions that every sales professional will recognise and in so doing we will remind you of the value, importance and significance of questions in selling.

Where do the ideas come from?

In short, from many years of selling in Barrie's case and many years of educating and studying people on my part. The ideas also come from our shared passion in helping to develop professional sales people and help to use our experiences and learning as widely as possible.

What is "Congruence"?

Looking at on-line definitions we come up with: agreement, harmony or compatibility.

The inception of the book and the learning that goes with it started in one of our conversations:

In answering the original question we posed:

"So where does the customer feature in this sales process?"

we began the debate and conversation that led to us recognising that a potential customer follows a "Buying Process" and that features so strongly in all the sales work we undertake with clients. From buying a loaf of bread to buying a new home, buyers will go through the same process; sometimes foreshortened and sometimes with repeated steps, but essentially, the process is the same. By aligning our sales approach with the customer's "Buying Process" we created the approach that is now recognised as a progression to "Congruence".

To explore this phenomenon we asked hundreds of people why they did or did not make a purchase. Analysing the responses we checked out the results with small groups of people and established that there was a buying process and indeed the need for "Congruence" in a successful sales situation.

Please note that references to he, salesman or any other gender specific term is used for ease of reading and, unless in a specific anecdote or quote, may be regarded as equally applicable to female as well as male.

THE ERA OF CONSOLIDATION

In which we explore professional selling in the United Kingdom in the middle of the last century and in which product integrity, values, belief systems and Beliefs, Attitudes, Skills and Knowledge are explained.

Background of the era

The early 1960's was a very different time from now in so many ways! The Second World War had been over for many years but life was not full of riches, cars were few on the road, people were careful with their money. The sixties were a time of change...the swinging sixties as rock 'n' roll gave way to popular music, The Beatles and the "Mersey" sound emerged. Along with West Coast music from the United States came a feeling that there was a bigger world. People started to take package holidays to the Mediterranean resorts.

Socially England was still emerging from a time of authority and command that was associated with the military times from not long before and the still prevalent social "class" system that still existed.

Life style improvements had started in the 1950's and historians will find the conservative Prime Minister's words, "You never had it so good" a forecast perhaps for the changes that the 1960's would bring. However there was not a surfeit of money in people's pockets and selling was tough in that sense. The average price of a house was just over two and a half thousand pounds! A loaf of bread cost the equivalent of five pence and the top rate of tax was 97.5%....in that top bracket the tax man took 19/6 (nineteen shillings and six pence) from every pound, leaving the equivalent of just two and a half pence for the earner (sixpence in old money!).

This was an era of consolidation and challenge in so many ways. Confidence and enterprise were growing and U.S. President Kennedy typified this by setting a target of landing on the moon before the end of the decade. So the 1960's saw the first man go into space (although the space-race was led by the USSR in this event) as well as the moon landings and man walking on the moon. In 1969 the skies saw the supersonic jet airliner Concord for the first time on a test flight. 1962 was the first time we could see live pictures from across the Atlantic via Telstar. In that same year there was another advance in entertainment with the cassette tape recorder becoming available. The forerunner of independent radio stations were the "Pirate" radio stations operating from ships in the North Sea. England was victorious in the world cup which was hosted in England in 1966. It was the next year, 1967 that was the time of colour television....yes we watched the world cup in monochrome (black and white).

Independent Television was in its infancy and advertising was just making a play in the homes of the nation. There were jingles that put particular products in mind and those who heard them could still recite them today, but how effective they were in driving sales may be unclear. What it did give was a platform from which the sales person could start.

Sales People were called salesmen in those times and PC only meant a Police Constable unlike today whence it has computing as well as "political correctness" connotations. A salesman often had a car, rare as they were, and may have been called a "commercial traveller" or a "sales representative". The commercial traveller was such a feature of the era that Morris, one of the main car manufacturers in England at the time, developed the Morris Traveller perhaps with the salesman in mind! Of course sales people worked in retail and many other static instances too but the internet, the contact centre and "sales channels" on television were not really even a glint in the eye of the most advanced thinker.

Consumers or "end customers" would buy mostly seasonal goods many of which were sourced relatively locally. Imports existed, but were generally expensive and "exotic" because the transportation costs were high. As far as consumables were concerned, the ability to import fresh produce at a reasonable price was still a pipe dream. Often, too people were much more engaged in home cooking and things we buy today as ready prepared would be an afternoon's work in the kitchen preparing, cooking and ultimately serving for dinner. The exciting and energising factor of the era was that people were beginning to see choice and were grateful for it. Previously choice had been limited, sometimes choice was not existent other than take it or leave it.

This was still an era where most people were conformist, having been through or seen the impact of a long lasting war and the sense of "control" or "authority" imposed upon a country. Yet to come was the "rebellion" of the youth of the day, some of whom were brought into a world where a ration book was needed to buy sweets at the local shop. Some of the changes they encouraged we will see manifest today in greater personal freedom and expectation, or even demand for certain things in life. As Bob Dylan heralded at the time in his song, "The Times, They Are A'changing".

Focus in this era

Much of the focus on sales at that time was on Fast Moving Consumer Goods (FMCG) and this provides us with a starting point for the progression towards "Congruence"

Companies selling Fast Moving Consumer Goods had the largest sales forces because at the time there were so many independent and individual retail outlets. They were keen to develop, learn and challenge sales methodologies. Much was learned by all salesmen from what was happening in FMCG. Other purchases took place for sure, and we will examine these as we go through the eras but considering the situation at the time the volume of sales and cash was in the FMCG arena.

Intriguingly the word "market" back then was more associated with local "barrow" markets or the larger "cattle markets" where farmers would buy and sell livestock and others would sell consumables to them. Where these markets existed there now stand shopping precincts or malls or vast multi-storey car parks. Often the barrow markets now are monthly affairs and called a "farmers' market" or similar and mostly locally produced foods are sold.

FMCG had an emphasis on the "F" and the "C" in that the consumables element meant that the goods would be used and need to be replaced or new purchases made. Things like toiletries perhaps were not so fast moving as a "cake" of soap (the term popularly used at the time) or a tube of toothpaste would last weeks, but other consumables like food, pet food, fuel, coal or coke were delivered home; drinks and so on were used at a faster rate. Especially food and drink as refrigerators were not installed in many homes which relied upon cool pantries or larders to store food. It requires little imagination to realise that dairy produce, fresh meat, fruit and vegetables were difficult to store safely and satisfactorily especially in high summer. So these, and tinned goods once opened to the "elements" were fast moving.

Thinking about the consumers' motivation and circumstances it is possible to understand why FMCG was so significant at the time. As people's wealth gradually increased and consumerism was in its infancy, people looked to make life more convenient and to take more time for themselves. FMCG was destined to fuel the convenience that became associated with the era of consolidation. Food was delivered in dried form, just adding hot water created a meal or a soup, frozen goods came alongside refrigerators with "ice boxes".....the freezer was still to come. Washing machines grew in popularity and a spin drier rather than a wringer (or mangle) appeared in many homes. Record players which could stack "discs" and portable transistor radios were all part of the FMCG background. So, in this, the beginning section of the journey to understanding more about buying, we are focused on FMCG as the "market" and to complement that we are thinking about the commercial traveller. Our focus is on what the commercial traveller was doing to sell to the retail buyer. As I mentioned earlier, this was really where the larger sales forces were employed and where the real focus on sales, sales training and sales developments took place. Whilst the nature and size of the sales force has changed, many of the key elements of selling (Behaviour, Attitudes, Skills and Knowledge) remain constant today.

Most of the "Behaviour" of the commercial traveller was to be a representative of the company. This had certain implications for the style of approach and the "sales techniques" required. We will look at this more in the subsequent section in which we look at the main things to be learned from the era of consolidation that can still be applied today.

Think of a representative, another term for the commercial traveller, and perhaps you have an image of someone who is the respectable representation of the company (or emerging brand). The retail buyer would have been quite demanding in many cases and would not be averse to contacting "head office" if the representative was not up to scratch.

A representative, as the name implies, was less of an independent being and more the "embodiment" of the company he represented. And selling; well if you know the client and his needs well enough it could almost be boiled down to "order taking". The magic was in ensuring there was an order to take.

Expectations and Motivations

So, what were the motivations and expectations of the salesperson AND the buyer back in the beginning of our journey? For the salesperson it seems to us that it was similar to today: achievement, recognition, reward, financial payment (wage and bonus), maybe a sense of "winning". Winning is an interesting one as it operates in different ways and different levels. It means winning orders, "landing" the customer and successfully getting business from them. Winning also means being better than colleagues, better than last month, better than target, better than your boss expects. All of these are healthy examples of a competitive person and are part of the make up of every successful professional salesman. Achievement comes from the sense of wanting to ensure that goals and targets are met. Salesmen are competitive and achievement is the realisation of that competitive spirit. Recognition for the salesmen here is based upon self recognition, that of the "management" and the buyer. Being recognised for what we have done is important to us all but perhaps is heightened by the needs of a salesman. Often recognition by ones-self of achievement is more than enough, but the external validation by managers and customers is great for most salesmen as it endorses the success they have achieved.

I have separated reward and financial reward (payment) as often I feel that the non-financial rewards are overlooked. By these I refer to the rewards of achievement, success, self congratulation, congratulation by others and the general psychological and emotional rewards that these things bring. Of course most people want the financial rewards too but I do see them as different.

What do we mean by motivation and how is it relevant here? Put simply this is the reason we do things. Some reasons are imposed; like laws, regulations, conformance, or we don't want to upset an apple cart. Other reasons maybe more personal or self centred: satisfaction, pleasure, happiness, freedom, independence. Others may be some kind of hybrid of internal and external but if we pushed we would trace them back to being either internal or external: reward, recognition, status, payment, achievement.

OK, some motivation or "reason for doing" something may be less intense than others but there is still something that compels us or drives us and here we will explore the salesperson's and buyer's motivations.

Let us elaborate upon the buyer's motivations as we really need to understand them well if we are to be successful in selling. This is not to diminish the expectations and motivations of the salesman, but understanding customers was something that has been fairly critical from the outset of our progression.

The buyer's motivation was that he wanted "product" to sell, to move along from his shelves as quickly as possible and with as much return as possible. His motivation was profit margin and cashflow. He needed to sell, and to sell with reasonable speed, to ensure his cashflow was positive and he was returning profit on the expense of the purchases originally. He would be lucky to have credit, so fast turn round became all the more important to ensure a positive cashflow and profitability.

With this in mind, the business buyer was keen to buy products which he knew were good "sellers" in his environment, represented value for money so he could appeal to his clientele and upon which he could still place a reasonable mark-up or margin to cover his own costs of operation and return a profit too. Interestingly, in this time of consolidation, new products were developed and brought to market. The salesman had to try and persuade his buyers to "try" the new products and see how they would sell in their environment.

Looking at the motivation of the end consumer was what drove the purchasing patterns of the buyer in a retail store and also drove his motivation. That in turn played back to the "trade" or wholesale salesperson who, if he was to be successful needed to match his motivations to those of the retail buyer. It may seem a trite truism but it is salutary to recall the basis of trading in these simple terms when we can so easily lose sight of it in today's electronic, instant and global markets. That basis has been pushed by marketing and advertising which was less prevalent in the 1960's but it is nevertheless still evident in today's merry-go-round of selling.

Bear in mind that at the start of our journey there were far more individual retail traders than today when we see super or hyper markets, chains owned by public limited companies and high streets populated by familiar names no matter where you go. Remember too the local sourcing of many consumables, the fact that consumers did not have vast disposable incomes and often indulged in home cooking and do it yourself (DIY) repairs, maintenance and development on cars, homes, clothing or gardens. So their motivation was often value for money, or even cheap products which served a purpose or fulfilled a need. Luxuries for most were a rarity and people tried to make "every penny count".

For most FMCG businesses at the time the motivation was straight forward; move good volumes in good time and cash flow and profitability would follow. Put this into the context of how much storage space there was, shelf space and or stock room back up as well as the refrigeration capacity or capability within the shop and the salesman had an idea of what he could and could not sell. "Lines" that may have sold well in other stores were a temptation to "push" elsewhere, but if that line, for whatever reason was not selling it was not one that would be attractive to the buyer. Whilst much of this process is now automated, motivations remain similar today for many organisations.

In essence the need to understand the business motives was and is crucial to success. What made success for the client led to success for our commercial traveller too. One thing we can all learn from this is that what may be important for me is not necessarily important for my client. Patience and understanding become qualities that are necessary if not the absolute driving forces we associated with selling in our BASK acronym (Behaviours, Attitudes, Skills, Knowledge) below.

Ignoring the client's needs and pressing on regardless was a temptation and patience would sometimes lead to frustration. However, trying to promote products or sell them where they were not wanted could be likened to pushing water uphill...tricky to say the least.

Brand

Compared to today, brand and the concept of brand were in their infancy in the 1960's. In a sense brands developed through popular use and familiarity. Certain product names emerged and some were already part of the average household vocabulary. Vacuum cleaners were pretty much known as hoovers and Hoover was the brand name of a particular vacuum cleaner. But consider that exposure of brand to a consumer market was still quite limited in that television (TV) advertising was still emerging and many homes did not yet have a TV or access to the "commercial" channels. Most advertising was about name recognition and some notion of differentiation from competitor products. Public gratitude for choice was only starting to emerge so recognition of a "brand" was in its infancy. Much of the recognition was reliant upon simple slogans that were memorable.

For example:

- You'll wonder where the yellow went, when you brush your teeth with Pepsodent!

- Don't for get the Fruit Gums Mum

- Ahhhhh Bisto

- A Mars a day helps you work, rest and play

- Trill makes budgies bounce with health

- Graded grains make finer flour

Interestingly several of these products still exist today. But from those early days these were simple but effective words that you could remember when you were in the shops.

But at that time brand was not as significant as we may think now. It was in the early stages of "mass consumerism" and drawing differences between one product and another. Brand at that time was mostly about recognition, it included presentation and perhaps, of the time, the significance of suitability and even "respectability".

Advertising could help the salesman if he mentioned to the retailer that a certain product had or was about to be advertised on T.V.

The key elements of selling

Here, and in each subsequent chapter we will explore the Behaviours, Attitudes, Skills and Knowledge that the successful salesman had to deploy. We refer to them as key elements as they were the fundamental basis of success and marked, in each era, the successful from the ordinary.

Having an understanding of where these take us in our search for "Congruence" is important as it reminds us that experiences help us learn. Many people will say something that amounts to "old is bad, new is good". That is not the case and even if we modify it to "old is irrelevant, new is relevant" we can still miss the point that the old stuff has helped to generate the new stuff and some of the old stuff is still important in what we do today. In fact many of the key elements of selling do not change radically; some may change with the times or take on a different emphasis. Some new things have emerged over time too but let's look at these later!

Most of the credentials for a successful professional salesman are outlined in four elements. We use the acronym BASK to show those elements as Behaviour, Attitudes, Skills and Knowledge. A quick view of those elements will give an understanding of how they related to the sales environment and show what is still relevant today. We'll address those elements that have been perennially important and in later eras we will develop and possibly add to them as "new" or developed Behaviours, Attitudes, Skills or Knowledge became relevant.

Behaviour

Put simply, this is what we do and to an extent how we do it. In the times of consolidation we had the basis of present day key elements although we may have added or modified the slightly. Back then the salesman's key Behaviours were:

- *Preparation*

Turning up at the wrong place at the wrong time and not having stock reports and so on would spell disaster. So preparation for each day and each client was essential. It is as true today as it ever was that preparation for a customer and the potential to sell is critical. The phrase "failing to prepare is preparing to fail" seems stark but it is true. If we put it in the context of the "commercial traveller" or representative of the 1960's preparation included being aware of the customer's motivation and also what was selling and what was not. The details of what the salesman needed to be aware of we will elaborate further in the paragraphs that follow, but being prepared and being aware were critical to success.

It is important to remember the disciplines that were instilled in this time by taking it in context that there were no emails, faxes or mobile phones let alone the current ability to have communication in multiple forms in a single hand held device. The salesman had to be prepared as there was no immediate back up from head office.

- *Awareness of customer*

Typical questions about his customers to which the salesman might need answers were: Who is he? What will motivate him? What is his target market? What will encourage him to buy more? What is his response to TV advertising of products he is likely to retail?

Here we are referring to the customers' motivation for buying and selling particular goods. As we described earlier, for the most part in our example this would be quick sales for turnover and profitability.

It is difficult to cite every example but awareness and preparation would be useful in all circumstances:

- A regular client who knows exactly what has sold and what are current stock levels

- A newly opened business starting to sell FMCG on a new housing estate

- A regular client who is really "great" with all of his customers but has no administrative process or "systems" to follow

- Introducing a new product to an existing client who is very cautious about what his clientele will purchase

- Starting out with a set of clients / customers where you are new but they are regulars for the company you represent

One common theme that emerges is being aware of the *person* you are dealing with. The logical and organised client may present different opportunities and challenges from the chummy but disorganised character. Another theme that emerges is that of understanding the client's *market place.* What is the environment in which he is selling? Who are his customers? Is there an age profile or other social factor that may impact what sells or what is sellable? How well do you know what may or may not appeal to his customers? Note that these questions are as relevant to ask yourself if you are selling directly to "end users" or consumers.

• *Respectfulness*

This may be a slightly clumsy word but the essence of it is about being respectful to the client, his needs, his premises and his time and so on. It may also include the courtesies and manners of the day. Certainly in this era it included our commercial traveller wearing a hat and raising it to the client and his staff. It would also entail informing the client if a "replacement" or new commercial traveller would be visiting and where possible this should include introductions.

- *Time Management*

Being a representative on the road all day the salesman had a number of scheduled calls to make. To meet these would help him achieve his targets and would also keep his customers happy. Organisation and personal time management were key. This would often entail the commercial traveller driving to the furthest part of his "territory" to start the day and work his way towards home. Starting at nine o'clock at the extremity of his territory, the organisation achieved more calls from its representatives.

- *Reliability*

Perhaps allied closely to time keeping and respectfulness, the commercial traveller was expected to turn up on a regular basis and at a particular appointed time. If the visiting cycle to a particular client was the third Thursday of the month at 9.30 a.m. then that is the time one had to appear or else! To the buyer the salesperson *was* the company.

- *Record Keeping*

This primarily concerned the salesman recording as much information about the client or customer as possible. Such details as opening times, when the decision maker was present (or took his days off) were recorded. There was no contact database that so many people rely on today. The salesman built his own data sources and could share these with the company.

- *Reporting*

Reporting took time and was often built up from "card index" files of information. The reports included information about the local market conditions, competitors and sales volumes. Organisations were dependent upon the accuracy of the salesman's reporting.

Attitudes

In simple terms these are the expression of values and beliefs by which we lead our lives and which are usually "visible" in our Behaviours. For example a "couldn't care less" Attitude will be reflected in poor time keeping or lack of preparation and would result in inaccurate reports and so on. This Attitude may also be visible in terms of smartness, cleanliness, the travelling salesman's car, supplies of samples and general appearance. In the times of consolidation, we identified seven key Attitudes (still just as important today) that made salesmen successful:

◆ *Positivity*

Having a "can do" / "will do" Attitude separated the successful from the 'also-rans'. This also translates into self belief and confidence, without which a salesman may get some orders but will not be top of the pile. Positive Attitudes are also the basis for the successful Behaviours displayed by professional salesmen.

◆ *Focus*

Staying in touch with what is important to individual clients and not being distracted by trivia or interruptions was critical. Being polite and accepting the cup of tea may not have helped the focus. Focus is about being attentive and considering detail and not wandering off into simple distractions.

◆ *Competitive*

In essence this encapsulates the fact that sales people want to win and are often bad losers. A competitive salesman is one who will not want to lose. Be warned however that it does not necessarily translate into meaning an aggressive salesman and note that "aggressive" does not appear in our successful Attitudes list

Whilst it is not a sport, a healthy Attitude towards winning, gaining the sale, being top dog in a team each helped a successful salesman

This is not about sulking or not enjoying someone else's success but about not enjoying the feeling of losing. So it helps to drive the winner Attitude

- *Strong*

Inevitably there will be some "knocks" on the journey and a successful salesman cannot be deterred by a few setbacks. This includes determination which, like strength, is the Attitude that will pull a salesman through to success. We may consider this as being a form of resilience. To succeed in any walk of life it is imperative that we can take the brickbats and rise above them and continue, learning from mistakes but not allowing them to defeat us

- *Realistic*

This may almost seem a contrast to the positive competitor but being realistic is critical to success. By setting overly tough personal targets or goals or by trying to close sales that really don't work in the customers' interests may work once or twice, but being realistic about what will work leads to more frequent and greater success

- *Ambitious*

That said, the ambitious salesman will be one who tries to push the boundaries of reality rather than be completely constrained by them. One may refer to an ambitious salesman as being hungry. A hungry salesman is one who always believes that there are more sales to be made and rather than resting back on his laurels when targets are met, the hungry one will go for more

◆ *Divine Discontent*

This refers to a personal feeling that "I could have done more" or that "I didn't get it all right". It is about self criticism or personal dissatisfaction, but for it to work the salesman needs to remain strong and positive. This quality, if not tempered by the others can lead to the end of a sales career, but if tempered by the others is a great spur towards greater success

Skills

Skills are the things that we can do. They are more easily taught than Behaviours and Attitudes and so most training will focus on Skills or Knowledge. There were seven identifiable key Skills of success back in the times of consolidation which are still success criteria today:

◆ *Interpersonal*

In this changing time it was important to learn how to "deal" with a range of people in a different way. Under this heading we consider social Skills, communication and engagement of clients and customers. Fundamentally this is about an individual's ability to get on with others, to hold a conversation, to be polite, to feel at ease and to make others feel at ease and to establish a comfortable, positive atmosphere

As we said already, society was changing and the salesman had to address a number of social "airs and graces" or social events and "norms" that may not have been previously experienced. It was changing from an authoritarian community to more of a laissez-faire or relaxed and informal society

Writing and clarity of "message" were requirements. Getting the order right and reporting and recording progress were all significant

Strange when we think of the proliferation and ubiquity of the mobile phone, but the household and office phones were unfamiliar then and people needed to develop the skill in using them effectively

- *Control*

It may not always be possible to control a customer or their thinking, but the commercial traveller had to remain in control of their own thoughts and actions and through that "lead" a conversation in the direction of what they were selling. As we will see in the Knowledge section, the significance of knowing one's own products is critical. Control in a way would ensure that they were mentioned and elaborated in the conversation. It also had elements that we would see in more sophisticated terms these days and now would be referred to as "body language"

- *Questioning and Listening*

A precursor to this was to have good communication Skills. The buyer would have expected the salesman to make a lot of the conversation and provide a large amount of information, including industry trends and product Knowledge.

As the salesman of the time you would know a lot about the customer but it was critical to find out his needs, wants and motives and questions would allow this. Having asked, it was fundamentally important to listen and it may seem obvious today but the significance of listening was not always appreciated in the era of consolidation. It was a time when people had been told what to do for long enough and listening was "selective". The successful had to select to listen to his customer.

The formal process, which need not be "stiff and starchy" (there is room for personality and individuality in how it is delivered) has a similar structure from its opening to its close. It opens with some kind of welcome, greeting or introduction. Back in the era and the FMCG approaches it may have been something like:

"Well John / Mr Simpson (as appropriate to the relationship), it's time to look at what you need and how we can help you with sales for the next couple of weeks."

Nothing more complex than that but it set apart any social chit chat that may have preceded and brought both parties back to the point. Remember our commercial traveller had many accounts and a busy schedule; he was responsible for his time management so he needed to keep things moving along fairly briskly.

◆ *Presentation*

Talking product with the client, especially introducing something new required a specific communication skill of putting across key messages effectively. We have already described our focus in the era of consolidation as being FMCG and that the salesman was a representative of his organisation usually in this context. Usually the client was a single owner, perhaps manager of an individual store. This meant that "presenting" the products, services and offers to the client were usually in a one to one meeting.

It is often thought that such a presentation may be informal and "cosy" but it is important to remember that any sales presentation has to have some degree of formality and seriousness. The key thing here is that presenting to one person is rather different from presenting to two or more. For a start you only have to influence one person and all being well you are speaking to the decision maker in the one to one scenario.

As a relationship develops the salesperson finds the level of formality that is appropriate but as we said before, some semblance of formality is always important. It keeps the whole thing on a professional footing and allows the process to work in such a way that there is less room for misunderstandings and misinterpretations. Like all sales approaches, the more agreement that can be achieved in the small things on the way to the ultimate close the better and easier it becomes.

♦ *Objection Handling*

Usually the objection was about price and its impact upon profitability; changes were often not an option.

In the early days of selling objections were often tackled head on either by agreement (yes, we are expensive) defence (this is why we're expensive) or even attack (you don't seem to understand.... this is the reason why....). As may be seen, these may not have been too successful and may have led to protracted conversations.

♦ *Closing*

Partly this may have been trial and error for many sales people who were not always aware that the customer was ready to buy. The more successful were ensuring a buying mood that would lead to a conclusion (close) of the sale.

Closing a sale has many mystiques and legends attached to it and there are many techniques which it is not our purpose to describe here. Whether it be an assumptive close, a half nelson, a Duke of Wellington or whatever is not really material here. If you have established need and checked agreement and understanding along the way the close follows comfortably and naturally. It may be as simple as a statement:

"I'll put in an order for you then Mr Simpson, for the following..."

Or it may be

"Is that everything Mr Simpson? If so I just need your signature to complete the order"

Interestingly the notion of creating a buying mood may be retrospective but what it entailed was helping the client to be in a frame of mind where he was more likely to concentrate and be receptive buying. A buying mood is not necessarily about a candle lit ambience, but it has that level of significance. A sad truth about people is that we are all easily distracted and if our mind can easily butterfly to something else it will. Another sad truth is that we cannot concentrate on one thing for too long before needing some level of distraction....no matter how small or short lived.

Given time constraints and the importance for both salesman and client in concluding business effectively and efficiently it was always important to have the closing elements of the sales process conducted in an uninterrupted fashion. The buying mood in this instance would normally be undisturbed, brief as possible, factual, to the point and straightforward. Possible disturbances and distractions needed to be avoided as much as possible.

In simple terms this meant that the salesman should not try to close the deal or discuss detail if the client was still in operational mode or courteously making a pot of tea. The idea of waiting so there could be a shared focus was critical. Techniques at the time included thinking about where you parked your car so you would not be interrupted by someone seeking to move the "Morris Traveller"..... or the Ford Cortina!

◆ Positioning

Some folks believe that tomorrow's hello begins with today's good bye. Positioning was largely that and coupled with Behaviours and Attitudes already mentioned, it was about ensuring the customer knew when the salesman would next appear or when the goods may arrive. In some respects it could be seen as relationship management in its infancy.

Knowledge

This is about the facts, the stuff we know about. It is usually the sort of thing that quizzes test. Like Skills, Knowledge can be taught but sometimes, like Skills, we don't all take all of it on board. The retention and use of the following, basic but fundamentally important Knowledge items led to success back in those times of economic consolidation and are still just as relevant today.

• *Product Knowledge*

A thorough Knowledge of the products that the commercial traveller or representative was selling was essential. An understanding of the concepts of features, advantages and benefits also applied.

Most people will recognise the importance of product Knowledge and being able to use that Knowledge to help the customer decide that it is right for them. This, in the circumstances of our example could include the amount of stock that would occupy what amount of shelf space as well as details of the product itself.

Knowledge of the proposition encompasses more and in our example may have included things such as terms, credit options, assistance with stocking shelves, promotions, pricing, advertising, posters and so on. This fuller picture of what the salesman's organisation provided would be termed these days as the added value. In short and regardless of time they constitute and overall proposition which goes well beyond the direct product.

These value added elements were often differentiators in their day, but like all differentiators were often copied. However, knowing what your organisation had to offer above and beyond the product was often critical to a sale and maintaining a client

- *Competitors Products*

This Knowledge may not be so detailed but clearly if the customer started to talk about competitors it was important to be knowledgeable and be able to compare and contrast if necessary. This emerged as more and more important as choice grew.

- *Market Knowledge*

A broader awareness of the market conditions, what was selling, what was not popular, what consumers were thinking and the significance of emerging advertising campaigns was important

In this era the salesman was the fount of Knowledge and had to be believable as the buyer would use this Knowledge to develop and shape his business. We will return to these themes later in more detail and with relevance and reference to today's selling in the era of realism, where the buyer can check facts for themselves on the internet.

Reflections

Here we will explore the significance of what we have talked about and why it makes a difference to whether people buy or not. In many respects this is looking at what was going on between sales people and customers and the effect of the BASK elements.

We still hear the adage that 'people buy from people' and to an extent that is true. We also hear of hard selling and we also know that some sales are easier to complete than others.

To be honest, the customer was not always top of mind in this era other than being necessary in order to make a sale which was often targeted in terms of volume. It was necessary to understand motivations and so on merely to achieve the target of taking orders and where possible influencing new sales.

Hindsight is a wonderful thing and a reflective nature both a blessing and a curse. If we look back to what was happening in that era of consolidation we can see that changes were taking place in the customer's perspective and gradually they were becoming more selective as choice grew and as sales people we had to change our Attitude towards selling. It became less about reordering and more about choice and selection.

Trying to determine what was important for the customer may not have received the greatest consideration but it was apparent and has led to some of the new approaches we have adopted in selling now. So with the benefit of hindsight and reflection we can see that customers had more of a place than being "necessary recipient" or "order placers". Subtly we were learning that to be successful certain prerequisites were necessary.

The key is *awareness*. It covers a multitude of actions and areas but it typifies what sales people needed then and what they need now. Of course in our example we are talking of a relationship that may have built up over months or years and that may not always exist. In the case where it does exist the salesman must be cautious that familiarity does not impede the process and create assumptions. *'Mr Jones always buys a box of X so I will place that on the order to start with.'* Assumptions at this stage can be deadly so avoid them. Unfamiliarity with the client has an advantage that we will have to prepare and become aware.

Part of the awareness was to know what the customer was selling and that anticipated profit making. One common thing that many FMCG sales people did at that time was to check stock or inventory themselves quickly and make sure they had good tracking of what was selling and what was not moving. Remember this was in the days before bar codes and Electronic Point of Sale (EPOS) technologies were evident. This meant that reporting and recording were critical on a "by hand" basis. Much of this is done automatically these days but being aware and having done your homework before arriving with a client was an important discipline then and it is today!

So *what* we do to be prepared or aware may have some differences now from then but the principles still apply. Selling business to business or business to consumer may breed different approaches but awareness and preparation are critical.

For anyone to make a decision about anything they need to be informed unless they are so cavalier that any decision is thought to be a good one. So the customer needs to be informed. In the era of consolidation remember data and information was nothing like as free flowing or available as it is now. Hence our salesman had a range of responsibilities for informing the customer or bringing things to his awareness.

Perhaps the more astute were also more aware and did have information but even then they may not have had the whole picture. The salesman had the responsibility to ensure the client (in this example a retail grocery shop owner / manager) was aware of sales volumes and turnover of specific products by the stock checking and controls of record keeping and reporting. In some senses this was an administrative duty, now replaced largely by Electronic Point of Sale (EPOS) and similar tools. It may also be seen as part of a service that was provided to the customer.

Where sales and service have often been seen as opposite ends of a rainbow, this reflective insight shows that sales and service may well be on a continuum and that for a customer one cannot exist without the other. We mentioned the facts of convenience in terms of consumables but convenience was also important in terms of the service that buyers received. At the time the term "hassle" was nowhere near being as widely used as it is today but what was beginning to emerge for our clients was the idea of hassle free business. It was a sort of "Make it easy for me and you will be a real asset to me" relationship that began to emerge. Interestingly this began to become part of a customer's choice.

No matter where it begins or where it goes, all successful sales people have a process. The efficacy of the process depends upon how it is constructed and how engaged the customer is in the process but it is important to have a structure. We have discussed preparation and the importance of the formality of the presentation process. One thing that soon emerges and that you may have experienced or witnessed is that there are few customers who appreciate being spoken at, lectured or preached to.

An important part of a sales process, no matter what the salesman already knows, is asking the customer questions. This not only helps them to engage, but properly constructed and well thought out questions can also check the customer's understanding and allow us, as sales people to repeat or re-emphasise as necessary. Questioning and listening have developed over the years but at the simplest level our experience reinforces the importance of salesmen asking questions.

Many salesmen develop a sales "patter" which seems to work, but is often based upon informality and familiarity. The maxim behind this is that if I am relaxed and casual with my customers, if I talk "their" language, if I can be chatty with them I am more likely to win sales. That approach was probably more prevalent and successful in the era of consolidation than it would be today, but we soon learned that even then, a degree of formality and structure really helped. The social stuff could happen after the sale was complete, or in the greeting, but business was, is and always will be business and deserves its own place and time.

The process would include some kind of agenda which set out the structure of the next few minutes, engaged the customer and gained the first agreement. It was probably something like:

> *"What I'd like to do is just review what has been selling well, what new opportunities exist, introduce a new product that I am sure you will like and see what you want to order. Is there anything else that you want to talk about? How is that?"*

Then there was the factual bit and the opportunity to ask questions and really engage the customer.

Our salesperson in that era also had to ensure his client was aware of new products and their potential in the client's selling domain. As part of the hassle free element of the relationship it was almost a part of the salesman's role to be market aware so he could share that awareness with the client too. The client could then use this awareness to impress and influence his own customers or other decision makers.

Data needed, as ever, to be presented as information. In other words the data needed to tell or show a meaningful story to enable the client, the decision maker to make a decision and to feel confident that it was based upon a sound foundation and not just a "gut feeling" that this or that may sell. Data as information and telling a useful story is as important today as it was then...perhaps more so as we are flooded with data from so many sources.

Whilst there was not a symbiotic or even parasitic relationship between client and salesman, the good salesman was making himself useful and valuable to the client. To say that a salesman could become indispensible is possible but is perhaps a far less likely expectation today. But clearly the client would and did benefit from hassle free information and an aide in making useful decisions. Although that relationship has changed in many ways over time, the basis of what a client or customer expects is clear to see.

It was also important for our salesman to be aware that ultimately the decision of what or if to buy rested with the client. It would have been easy to presume a power in the relationship as the salesman because you had the information. It would have been easy to have written out an order and have the client sign it....and that did happen. However for sustained success it was fundamental to inform and enable the client to be the decision maker and buyer. Respect and honour were increasingly important whilst trust was becoming more and more significant. Our Behavioural notion of "respectfulness" was strongly in play here. This was true too with customer choice as, albeit they were grateful for choice, with greater awareness came the need for salesmen to sell.

Armed with the reports and recordings of stock information, without "correcting" the customer, it would be possible to check awareness, understanding and help move the conversation in a positive direction. It may begin with a question such as:

"What has been selling well Mr Simpson?"

Or perhaps

"What have your customers been most interested in?"

Building the picture of sales together and "playing" to the client's motivation and need for fast turnover and profitability the salesman would focus on the faster movers and the profitable sales. He would have the opportunity to introduce new products that matched the client's needs and helped to fuel his motivation.

So the conclusion of the facts section might be something like:

"So you have made a lot of sales of tinned goods and flour seems as popular as ever. Soups and baked beans have been the most popular items so we need to replenish those well. So the items I have on my list are....."

For many that might be called a summary or conclusion, but it is not quite the close of the sale yet.

If there are new products to introduce, it was normal practice to close the initial sale before adding something new. That way there was no dilution or confusion. It may be built upon existing sales and popular products and initially may be at an introductory level. Where a link to existing sales could be made that was advantageous but it should address the client's needs primarily. For example it may be something like:

"I wanted to introduce our new margarine product Mr Simpson. We have noticed a lot of customers are buying margarine alongside flour to use in their baking. With your high level of flour sales it will probably interest your customers too. Let me tell you something about it and see if you think it may be of interest..."

As an aside to the sales process there needs to be the recognition that sometimes a customer objects on some grounds or another; price, volume, stock control or whatever it might be. In the era of Consolidation objections were handled but not necessarily very effectively, often resulting in protracted conversations between customer and salesman. Objection handling Skills have dramatically improved but also reflect the changes in customer and salesmen relationships.

Consumers at that time had grown from the earlier era of rationing but were still generally cautious in what they bought and how much they spent (something we as salespeople should always bear in mind). They were also used to "black market" sales by people often referred to at the time as "wide boys". Reliance on the black market for some things may have still existed but for the most part in this era of consolidation more things were available through formal or open channels.

Decisions to buy were not taken lightly or without some consideration and the more mutual respect and trust that were evident in a relationship the more successful it could be. Recognition of who was the decision maker and whose money was at stake were often quite critical to the success of a sale. It was also important to recognise and address the motivations of the buyer.

Whether or not the motivations were related to ego or status is a moot point but it does not alter the need to address them. As a shop owner the need to sell goods quickly and as profitably as possible could not be ignored. If it was ignored then sales would drop, trust and respect would dwindle and the relationship could transfer to someone who would address the shop owner / keeper's underlying needs and motivations.

The basic motivation derived from the business was the same but there was always a different edge to the motivation of the owner or self employed "proprietor" of a business. Managers or employees had incentives but were probably less ambitious or hungry than an owner. Business owners were in character closer to the salesman (or a good salesman anyway) than managers or employees.

The owner, as today, had a vested interest that was much more directly related to the results of sales performance and cash flow whilst the employee or manager generally would have been more cautious and careful.

Beyond the immediate business needs of cash flow and profitability, if a salesman was able to understand the client's personal motivations they could help them fulfil those ambitions too. It may only be conversational but helping the customer to keep in mind the holiday, new car, extension to the business premises or a change around the home could encourage them in their buying, and selling of the FMCG goods that the salesman was selling to them. So understanding the individual, where they fitted in the business and, especially if they were the owner, what the personal motivations were was a help.

An important thing to bear in mind here is that to keep business, gain repeat business and referrals, it was critical to remain ethical and not to "peddle" goods that the client was not going to be able to sell. Equally, though many salesmen do not like to be inhibited by rules it was important to maintain the selling company's integrity and status by adhering to such aspects as invoicing, credit, discounts and delivery timescales.

This may seem obvious, but it was crucial to ensure that the features and benefits of the product *and* proposition were aimed at the client's motivation. Bear in mind that our example is really wholesale selling to an intermediary so it is not the direct feature and benefit of the product to the consumer or end user that is of interest here. It was important to help the client realise this and to provide some assistance with the features and benefits for him to convey to his customers.

Our chief concern was to show how these products, and any added value we put with them, would enable the client to move product quickly and profitably. The concept of product flying off the shelf was important and the features had to address this benefit to the client.

It may seem a fairly basic step in selling that features (some would then add advantages) and benefits are important. What is more significant here is realising the different "level" or style of feature and benefit we are talking about and to whom it was addressed. So part of this understanding is about knowing to whom you are selling (not the end consumer in this case) and what *their* requirements and motivations are. You will see that this subtlety increases in importance as we progress on the journey and travel through different selling situations.

What we so often find in sales is that the true motivation is not revealed and therein lies the problem in converting certain sales.

Another key aspect of managing the situation with the client is that of creating a buying mood. That covers a whole spectrum of things but not least of them is creating a situation where focus and the absence of distractions can be achieved. It is interesting that our true focus or span of attention to a specific task is quite limited. It will vary but it is unlikely to be in excess of forty minutes before we seek some distraction (making a coffee, reading something, playing solitaire or whatever). True concentration and focus on detail is even less, some evidence suggesting that it may only be a few seconds! As we said before the practical early lesson of the era of consolidation was to park the car sensibly away from the shop you were visiting. The bigger issue behind that is ensuring that the customer or client can focus attention on you and what you are selling or discussing with them.

If there is any opportunity to be distracted many people will follow it and be distracted; the responsibility we have as the salesperson in this instance is to ensure we are not distracted either. There are many things we need to think of to ensure we are not disturbed; parking of the representative's car being our example here. We also need to do our best to ensure the buyer or client, is not disturbed either! A short burst of attention will allow the business to be done. If we need a long time we need to think of how we can introduce variety into the conversation so that attention can move around but remain purposeful and on target. These days the temptation is the power-point slide show or a plethora of visual aids. Useful though they may be we urge that you use them judiciously and to support a discussion not dominate it. Such tools were not really available in the era of consolidation.

Another aspect of the relationship that emerges is that of respect. We hope and trust that this is not seen as an old fashioned quality, even though we all acknowledge that respect may have changed in detail. Respect is multi-tiered and part of the continuity from the era of consolidation is the respect of another's time and space. Whilst we are very aware from the above that concentration or attention may be short lived, we can be equally aware that we should respect the time of the buyer. A simple and selfish reason for this may be that the buyer will be distracted if time is not respected.... "I have other things to do or get on with" is a big distraction.

In short one may say that the salesman learnt not to "outstay his welcome". Also it was important to respect the other person's space...not necessarily in the body language sense of personal space but that the salesman was on the client / buyer's premises and therefore should not take liberties.

This sensitivity that the buyer / client has certain time and space needs is an element of respect that will help the salesman establish a successful contact with their client. It may be better described as awareness of the client but the essence is that as sales people we learned and need to retain the concept of respect for our client.

If we think about motivations, the importance for the client simply translates right the way through to achieving his ambitions. For the salesman the importance of the relationship or human interaction is that it results in a sale and all that that means. Ultimately, without the interaction and the understanding and building of it there is no sale and neither party can achieve their ambition or motivation. Interpersonal, social and communication Skills have developed in style and methodology over time but remain fundamental to successful selling.

From the salesperson's point of view there is a fundamental here that means the difference between a sale, a quality sale or no sale at all. The expression "putting yourself in the customer's shoes" is probably quite commonly stated but not always truly understood or enacted. If we are able to place ourselves in the customer's shoes and see things from their perspective, then as a salesman we can be at an advantage because we can establish a relationship with them more easily.

Very often people refer to the concept of rapport. In our experience rapport is often misunderstood as being the same as friendly, jocular, chummy or just chatty with the customer. This is not what it means in our understanding, although in some circumstances that may be appropriate. Rapport is about being on the customer's wavelength and establishing more than just chattiness. It is about awareness, ensuring no interruptions and respecting the client's time and space (at least). Rapport is a theme to which we will return as it becomes increasingly important and has many aspects that we will develop.

Put simply it is fundamental to both parties to establish a relationship so that both their needs can be met. Some relationships do not work because there is a lack of understanding or awareness between the two parties. Some relationships form quickly, others benefit from longevity and the building of mutual understanding or awareness.

It makes a difference to both parties if the relationship exists or not.

Part of our purpose here is to make you stop and think. Many of the basics you know well and can apply in your sleep. That may be a problem in that when we do things on "auto-pilot" our attention and focus are often far more on ourselves and our processes than they are on the customer, his process, his needs, his motivation and as such we can often mismatch the features and benefits of a product or service.

Often we hear that a "Customer is King" only to find that in practice the customer is really either a nuisance, a necessary evil or a distraction. We hear too of customer-centric organisations which in reality do not have the customer in central focus; rather the Attitude may be "I have a green hexagon, who wants to buy a green hexagon? Madam, green hexagons are the answer to your problems!" OK this may be an exaggeration to illustrate a point, but it is a point is worth making. As individual salesmen we can decide how we approach our customers and what style we will use. If our style and approach are totally at odds with the organisation we work for we must choose what we want to do.

Anyway, we will return to the value of the lessons we learned in the era of consolidation and relate them to how we see successful selling in this, the information or realism era.

A summary

It was a time of consolidation after a period of austerity. People were becoming aware of choice. It formed the foundation of what we know and how we sell today but things have changed.

FOCUS IN THIS ERA

In this era we used the example of Fast Moving Consumer Goods.

Motivations and Expectations

Looking at the customer and his point of view as we focus on FMCG and the retail environment of the local grocery shop we find the customer needed to make a profit and needed to turnover his stock relatively quickly in order to have a good cash flow. The salesman needed to be sensitive to those needs.

Brand

At the time brand mostly related to advertising and brand awareness. The days of TV advertising were in their infancy and mostly advertising was about helping us choose one brand over another as choice grew.

KEY ELEMENTS OF SELLING

Behaviours

The key Behaviours we would emphasise as still relevant now but were apparent in this time are:

- Preparation

The importance of being ready for the meeting and all that that entailed

- Respectfulness

Showing respect for the customer, his premises and his time

Attitudes

Having a positive, focused Attitude is still as important today as it was in the era of Consolidation

Skills

The Skills we emphasise in this era which have a great impact upon today's selling ability

- Interpersonal

The ability to get on with people and put them at their ease

- Questioning and Listening

Conversation as well as drawing out the needs by careful questions and good listening

- Closing

The ability to ask for the business and not leave it in doubt that you want the order and the ability to minimise interruptions at the key moment

KNOWLEDGE

There is considerable Knowledge that has a bearing on our ability to sell including products, competitor products and the market in general

REFLECTIONS

In this section we bring together all of the above in context and discuss why it was important and significant.

The Parable of Les March
as told by Barrie Smith

Leigh-on Sea in Essex, was in the 1960's a haven of high rise buildings housing elderly affluent individuals living in apartments. Many of these individuals, denied by leasing restrictions of the company of cats or dogs were the proud owners of caged birds – normally Budgerigars or Canaries.

In this high rise conurbation nestled a small, tired grocery shop – one man and his assistant.

So it was that I made a sales call on this shop accompanied by my sales manager in his role as motivator, coach, trainer and inspiration.

The purpose of the call was to obtain an order for our products which ranged from flour to dog biscuits to bird seed and to specifically focus on our promotional product – Tydisan, a sand papered product that was placed on the bottom of bird cages thus enabling the pet owner to clean the cage without resorting to newspaper.

Our visit proceeded normally and we had obtained our order for the products normally stocked by this establishment.

Now for the promotion product sale!

I took a sample of the Tydisan product from my brief case and proceeded to begin the sales presentation.

Immediately our grocer interrupted – "Son" he said, "I am a high class grocer, I have specialist cheese, I grind my own coffee and cure my own bacon"

I looked around the store and, masking my incredulity with a polite nod of my head in acquiescence I responded – "I understand that Sir, and I am sure that your clientele, living in their luxury apartments, on Sunday mornings, when they refresh their budgies cage do not want to screw up a soiled copy of the local newspaper. Rather" – and here using finger and thumb I held up my sheet of Tydisan – "they would prefer to take out a soiled Tydisan sheet and drop it into their waste receptacle". At this point I let go of the Tydisan and it dropped into the waste bin in the grocer's emporium.

Today I would recognize this as the point of "Congruence" when the grocer and I were in aligned and in harmony – then I just thought "Got Him"!!

We both knew the sale was made but I was just about to learn a salutary lesson for both sales professionals and sales managers – always insist that in the sales presentation the sales manager always remains silent. Never allow them to do any more than say Good Morning or Good Bye unless you have agreed something different prior to the call.

At the very moment when my high class grocer had made the decision to expand his range of high quality merchandise my sales manager, Leslie Charles March, ex Lyons Tea Van Salesman and my 'inspiration' delivered his contribution to the presentation,

"After all Sir, the modern grocer is only like a bloody hardware store"

I picked up my Tydisan sample, placed it in my briefcase, closed the case, shook the grocer's hand, thanked him for his order and left.

Back in the car Les and I started the normal de-brief of the call – it was the shortest one I ever had, "Sorry mate – I mucked that up for you didn't I?"

(A comment from Kieran: Note that Barrie's thought of "Got him" was absolutely how salesmen approached life in those days. Today's seeking of "Congruence" shows how far we have come as a profession).

THE ERA OF EXPANSION

In which we explore the impact of greater choice and customers beginning to flex their buying "muscles", the response of professional sales people and how customer choice and bargaining power, brand development, product cycles and selling response are identified.

Background of the era

Having been through an era where new opportunities arose, in which a Prime Minister had heralded that the population had "never had it so good" there had to be a period of expansion. This built upon all the new opportunities and consolidation that had gone before. From being grateful for choice, consumers were faced with greater opportunities to buy and approached life with careful excitement.

The need and desire to expand was almost an imperative but consolidation had also created expectations and established security, freedoms and mobility that were impossible to deny. So whilst we may think of it as an era of expansion, it was certainly far from an era of stagnation. In fact the World Wide Web has its roots in the era of expansion as people (in that case Tim Berners-Lee) sought to make the most of new technologies and opportunities. Bill Gates was already "at it" as the early versions of the Windows software came to market.

T.V. at the time included some shows we may now be embarrassed to watch but at the time they provided great entertainment. For example Mork and Mindy, The Dukes of Hazard and The Muppet Show were amongst the popular viewing list along with Happy Days and Are You Being Served. A little later, programmes such as the Multi-Coloured Swap Shop or Newsround (originally known to many as John Craven's Newsround), Postman Pat or Magpie were popular to people of all generations.

Bright, energetic, cheery and colourful programmes were evident. Comedy still retained some of the satire that the era of consolidation had brought and generally there was a sense of freedom and a sense that one could speak one's mind and be open without harsh criticism. Consolidation had gradually replaced the post war era of austerity and conservatism (with a small 'c') and now was a time to expand on the liberalism (small 'l') that had been generated.

That liberalism emerged in many ways with the "Punk" movement in popular music and the strikes by many unions including miners, postal workers and dustmen. This led to the "winter of discontent" in 1979 and earlier to a three day week designed to conserve fuel and resources. These were not the easiest of times in some respects as people asserted their freedoms, independence and uniqueness.

A little later in this era we had events such as the Falklands War which seemed to create a huge upsurge in national pride; Prince Charles married Lady Diana Spencer, a commoner, as did his brother Prince Andrew in marrying Sarah Ferguson. Mobile phones appeared, although they were like bricks and the battery pack was immense. It was an era that introduced the expressions "yuppie" and Thatcherism to Britons and space hoppers were gradually replaced by BMX bikes. Life was still not as fast moving as it is today but the emergence of greater mobility and the start of multi-national, even global organisations, which had existed before, but with less prevalence and less movement of employees, brought changes of their own.

Music was not dominated by the Mersey sound any longer and Punk gave way to a New Romantic era and popular male artists wore makeup as part of their act. Adam of Adam and the Ants, Boy George of Culture Club were amongst the makeup wearers. The self confidence that had come through the era of consolidation was evident in so many as we moved into the era of expansion.

Convenience had moved on too and the introduction of the compact disk (CD) in this era was an indication of the continued pursuit of technology designed to make our lives easier, faster, more comfortable and perhaps safer. Entertainment and capturing the day were made easier by the camcorder replacing the super-eight or similar home movie kits. Disposable contact lenses gave some people a new sense of freedom and reduced the daily grind of cleaning lenses and ensuring their thorough hygiene!

The acceleration of change over the eras of expansion and consolidation were immense. When one looks back over the entire twentieth century it was a century in which many major inventions and "convenience devices" were introduced to the world. It was probably towards the end of the century that the speed of refinements and new applications of the earlier inventions was most noticeable.

Lifestyles were becoming easier for many people; holidays abroad the norm for many; wine was replacing beer as the nation's favourite tipple in the U.K. and probably at the end of the era of expansion, many people had more spending power than ever before.

Focus in this era

Our sector of business in this section is Capital Goods and more specifically I am referring to the sale of office furniture to a corporate buyer. I have mentioned that this buyer is operating in a very different environment and has different motivations from our FMCG proprietor.

Another of the differences that this sales orientation points up is that some sales are almost instant or at least "short-cycle" or short term. This style of selling is more long-cycle (longer decision times and longer delivery times...including a phase for manufacture possibly). An order may take several visits to the customer before it is placed, completed and all the attendant purchase orders and paperwork put in place. This will place a different pressure on the Behaviours or Skills of the salesperson as we will see shortly.

An essential difference in this sales environment is that the sale has to satisfy several people, several criteria and is probably going to come about through a group decision. While the purchasing may be delegated entirely to one person often there will be others who will want their say. Public sector purchasing, because it is using taxpayers money, may go through more rigorous balances and checks although it is not unique in seeking tenders and competitive bids right the way to final choice.

It may be thought that this sales environment is "third party" selling: the salesman sells to a buyer or purchasing board but another person ends up as the final user. This is an unusual sale, demanding techniques, accountabilities and sensitivities perhaps that FMCG selling had not required.

Because of the tendering and bid processing alluded to an above, it is evident that selling in this environment is also likely to require some element of negotiation. This is a skill which we will elaborate upon shortly. Given that there are a number of people involved, budgetary constraints, possibly more direct competition than in FMCG it emerges that negotiation can be a significant tool

Expectations and Motivations

As our "vehicle" for understanding the next stages in sales development and learning we are staying in a business to business context but shifting from consumer goods to capital goods. We are also shifting from a sale to a proprietor or owner of an individual shop to selling to a corporate buyer, responsible for a budget but also responsible for providing suitable capital goods to colleagues and his senior managers alike.

Motivations of this buyer are very different from the FMCG owner although there will remain some similarities. The similarities will be along the lines of getting value for money, not paying more than is necessary, ensuring delivery timescales are suitable and buying the appropriate (right) product, fit for purpose.

As an example here we will use the sale of office furniture to a corporate buyer. If we examine his role and position within an organisation we will find that he may not be at a senior level within a company, he has a delegated budget for replacement and renewal, he may have access to budget and funds on specific capital projects (for example an office move or expansion or the creation of a new team or an office refurbishment programme).

So from here, let's try to understand the motivations of a buyer. He has to satisfy the organisation's needs for supplying appropriate furniture within the budgets set. He has to ensure the furniture is functional and fit for purpose. Whilst he may not be too bothered about being liked or loved by colleagues he will try to ensure that they are at least satisfied that the furniture provided helps them to do their job. Comfort may again not be a top priority but discomfort may be counter-productive. So he has considerations for a wide range of people and a wide range of criteria like budget and appropriateness. He needs, therefore, to understand the needs of others and he needs to consider such concepts as value for money. That concept is interesting for the sales person too, because value for money and cheap, low cost are NOT the same thing.

Given the buyer or customer's motivation here does it change the salesperson's perspective? In short, yes it does. Now the salesperson has to meet the perceived or hidden motivation and requirements of others that he may not be directly selling to. He has to meet the overall budgetary and physical requirements of the organisation, provide the quality of practical, useful goods to the end user and maintain positive relations with the actual buyer. The salesperson's own motivations of a full order book had not changed but the means to achieving that goal had been substantially modified by the notion of selling to a corporate buyer rather than direct to a proprietor of a retail business.

It was during the era of expansion that the concept of *rapport building* seemed to take a greater significance. Clearly any salesperson needed to establish some form of relationship with their client over time, but it does take time and cannot be successfully achieved in minutes or even hours. True rapport is a deeper thing and builds in so many ways over time. Part of what a salesperson has to establish quickly is a professional relationship which may also be warm, friendly and approachable. Too often we see that rapport is associated with the friendly, warm and approachable side and that the professional element is ignored. There is almost a compelling sense that the salesperson has to build friendship, humour and informality as quickly as possible. Over time that relationship may work and be appropriate, but it may equally be damaging so it is important to start off on the right foot.

We will return to the theme of relationship building as part of the final section of this book, but our contention is that rapport is not instant although some kind of working relationship or "accommodation" may be fairly readily established. In the example here, the salesman is trying to establish a relationship that will endure AND he may have more people than just the buyer to contend with!

Brand

Brand had developed during the previous era from being a means of recognition and differentiation, mostly in terms of recognition, to being something that carried expectations on the part of the customer. Familiar purchases were made but the consistency and "quality" of the brand had to be present. Persil really had to wash whiter!

The understanding of brand in our expansion era context has to be on several levels or at least in several contexts. The considerations of brand has both physical and "emotional" aspects here: the physical is about quality, finish, fit for purpose and so on whilst the emotional aspect is about aspects such as being valued, portraying image and creating atmosphere or mood.

Let's start with the physical aspects of brand here. In our example of capital goods (office furniture) the physical attributes of a brand may be clear to see. We know that brands may vary and that there will be "top of the range" and ordinary quality. These differences however do not excuse the lower end ranges for being unfit for purpose or "shoddy" and ill-fitting. A buyer will understand the difference between buying solid wood or a laminated finish on chipboard or MDF. The expectation remains that a desk drawer will open and close, that it is lockable, that cupboard doors will fit, that work surfaces will be cleanable, reasonably durable, flat, blemish and snag free. The expectation is that solid wood to be more durable but that equally it will require different treatment to ensure its longevity or durability.

Seating somehow seems to become an emotive subject more readily, but staying with the physical side if it is adjustable it is expected that the adjustors will work, if it has wheels, or castors, it will move easily and if it is a swivel chair it is expected to swivel. The cloth wood, plastic or leather of the chair should be consistent, clean, cleanable, offer as much appropriate comfort as possible and so on. Some brand names may give me a greater sense of confidence that these attributes can be achieved and others may have a poor reputation, regardless of price, and these will have a big bearing on my decision in purchasing or not.

Beginning to cross the "divide" between the physical and emotional aspects of brand is the salesperson himself. We briefly mentioned the professional relationship but as yet we have said little about the image of the salesperson who may be representing the manufacturer directly or may be a reseller, acting on behalf of an agent that may or may not sell more than one manufacturer's goods. The salesperson, may be the embodiment of the reseller or the manufacturer.

During the era of expansion it was almost an unstated "law" that salespersons or representatives were smart, tidy and clean, wore suits or smart business clothes, had shiny and clean shoes and used "sales presenters" or brochures that were pristine and looked unused. This personal image was actually an important part of the branding of the selling organisation and in image terms created or maintained images of smart, professional, reliable and so on. Almost subliminally the image of the brand was being reinforced or, occasionally being eroded!

Emotive elements of brand were beginning to emerge in that what was represented by the quality and style of the products impacted users and their self perceptions.

Many people think of brand as the logo, the colour, the advertising or the product name. They are part of the brand but there is also the "emotional" side of brand, the subliminal messages of brand and the underpinning statements a brand may make through its people and the way they are treated, valued and represent the company or organisation for whom they work.

The key elements of selling

When we review the Behaviours, Attitudes, Skills and Knowledge required to sell in the Capital Goods, third party environment described above we will find that many are similar although some subtle changes and developments emerged. We have also seen that there will be a couple of new or additional Behaviours or Skills required to drive success in this new environment.

Behaviour

The subtle changes to Behaviours may actually be more than subtle in fact. However the theme of the Behaviour remains fundamental to the cause and pursuit of success. Let's look at them and amend and add any that are newly or differently relevant.

- *Preparation*

Preparation for any meeting and sale will remain important just as before. As this is a longer cycle sale preparation for each stage of the process is critical and the salesperson needs to be "on top of things".

- *Awareness*

We have possibly covered this already in the background, focus and brand sections. Suffice to say that the awareness of **all** people involved in the buying cycle was fundamentally important. We will explore the politics (small p) of this but they are significant.

- *Respectfulness*

This Behaviour remained significant throughout the eras and in the era of expansion it possibly expanded itself in that there were more people and situations of which to be respectful. This just served to emphasise the importance of respect.

◆   *Time Management*

We mentioned in FMCG that this was largely about keeping promises and keeping orders moving through as well as attending customer meetings on a timely basis. Those are both still true with Capital Goods but perhaps we should add the impressions created towards the brand by time keeping. To the buyer the salesperson *is* the company or organisation from which he is buying. How would things be if the salesperson was sloppy in time management? May the buyer start to think that production would be similarly sloppy (perhaps not just in timescales!)? Might he also be concerned that overall project timescales and cost overruns may occur?

In order that the buyer is confident that everything will happen on time and to plan, the salesman has to demonstrate an ability to manage time. His, as far as the buyer is concerned, will be the responsibility to progress chase orders put through....which could have fundamental consequences in the purchasing organisation.

◆   *Reliability*

This probably remains unaltered from the earlier Behavioural requirement but with the added perspective here of "brand image".

◆   *Recording*

It was still important to record but whereas before it was about stock, this was more about taking notes of meetings and keeping a good record of progress, requirements, who was involved, their individual perspectives and motivations and so on. It was not a feature of the era of expansion to have customer contact software, let alone sales force automation or comprehensive Customer Relationship Management systems so it was still an individual Behaviour.

◆   *Reporting*

Again there was probably less urgency attached to reporting as in the consolidation era or indeed FMCG sales, but it was tremendously important to keep management informed for purposes of planning, cash flow projections and, where appropriate purchasing materials and setting production schedules. Informal and formal in nature and style, the precise process of reporting would reflect the culture of the company, but whichever it was an essential ingredient of the process.

Because of the long-cycle nature of the capital goods sale we detected that some additional Behaviours may be required of the salesperson. Some of these may also impact Attitudes and Skills but it is appropriate to introduce them here.

◆   *Perseverance*

Some may also think of this as tenacity and it may also be very close to an Attitude. But persevering needs to be present for everyone's sake. If the salesperson becomes easily bored or expects instant results the chances of success become limited. To achieve a sale in this long term cycle it is fundamentally important to keep "on the case". In our example it is also critical to ensure that some form of project management throughout design, production and delivery takes place. In the eyes of the customer, the salesperson is the most likely contact point and so should take responsibility to ensure it all happens.

◆   *Patience*

Again this may work better if the Attitude is right, but the Behaviour of patience, calm, and acceptance that it won't happen quickly is important for the salesperson selling capital goods. One may think of this as an internal Behaviour whilst perseverance may be more overt. However, patience is crucial and needs to be shown. Decisions in this scenario take time and may well involve several people. The salesman cannot assume a quick decision or rapid progress at any stage and so his patience will be important for his own sake but also needs to be demonstrable to his customer and the entire "buying organisation".

◆ *Consistency*

This may be more critical than people realise. The consistency appears in so many ways and is essential if we are to establish any kind of long term relationship. It will be important that the salesperson is consistent in his messages and information. Lack of consistency will bring a question over trust and reliability. Also the selling organisation needs to be consistent throughout such that if the salesman is saying one thing it is backed up by "production" or "finance" for example.

Attitudes

Just as a reminder, our concern here is the Attitude of the salesperson on which they base their Behaviours and actions. These Attitudes are perhaps the personal driving force that keeps the salesperson going and from which they derive their success.

Where we introduced 'new' Behaviours of perseverance, patience and consistency we need to reinforce them by ensuring the salesperson has the right Attitude towards a longer-cycle sale. It is quite possible that a person can behave in a certain way (be patient... or appear to be at least) but the underlying Attitude is a mismatch. This may eventually cause a personal conflict of interest, the result of which is, usually, that the underlying Attitude will dominate.

It is possible that some Attitudes are apparently in conflict (hunger and patience for example) but provided they are genuine and the individual understands the significance of the situation, they are able to display the right Attitude and behave in a way appropriate to the customer or the sale.

The previous Attitudes of the salesperson remain which is fortunate as for the most part Attitudes stay consistent. Attitudes may change with experience and learning but generally Attitudes do remain with us for a long time if not for ever.

For the sake of completeness, but with no further elaboration here, the Attitudes that appear to drive success in sales are:

- *Positivity*

- *Focus*

- *Competitive*

- *Strong*

- *Realistic*

- *Ambitious*

- *Divine Discontent*

There may be a tempering or moderating effect of the patience, perseverance and consistency we have newly introduced in our new sales context, but other than that there are no modifications to make. The tempering effect may be more or less necessary in different sales scenarios, but in our build towards the concept of "Congruence" we would argue that the tempering is necessary in most sales scenarios, especially as we find customers becoming increasingly discerning.

Skills

As with the Behaviours and Attitudes there is little modification to the Skills needed to be a successful salesperson in this environment compared with the FMCG scenario. We need to recognise as salespeople that the general "social" environment does move on and the general mood of people changes. As we said in the background to the era of expansion it was a time when people had greater expectations, more disposable income and with those probably more discernment and demands.

Thinking too about our sales example here, the buyer whilst having certain restrictions and contrary demands placed upon him, he was likely to transfer the demands to the salesperson. His style might well be "I have to buy this within budget and I have to satisfy all these needs, so salesperson, what can you do?"

There are some new Skills that we added because of this progression and many of these would be described as "soft skills". That is not to denigrate them in any way as in fact it is often the presence of soft skills that differentiates the successful from those who do "OK" or less well.

Again there may well be an underlying Attitude that is necessary that feeds the skill and allows it to be successful and again some of the newly introduced Skills may be seen as contradictory to the original Skills. Let us assure you they are not contradictory but complementary although their addition may make the art of selling a shade more complex than it was before.

Our earlier and essentially unaltered list is:

* *Interpersonal (including social, communication and engagement)*

* *Control*

* *Questioning and Listening*

* *Presentation*

* *Objection Handling*

* *Closing*

* *Positioning*

The additional Skills which complement and build upon these start with empathy, part of interpersonal.

* *Empathy and sensitivity*

One might say this is all about understanding the buyer's motivation and that is not far wrong. However there are some more subtle 'things' going on here and an appreciation of the circumstances in which the buyer is operating may well be helpful. The salesman does not need sympathy in these circumstances (if he does maybe he needs to reconsider what he is doing!) but an awareness of the constraints, pressures, expectations and demands upon the buyer can help. Genuine empathy and sensitivity can help the salesman become a help to the buyer and ease the way through the minefield. The more the salesman and buyer can establish genuine 'connectivity' the more likely they can take almost a joint approach.

This takes time to establish and is probably what we may refer to as genuine rapport. This element was a fundamental learning and connects directly to our notions of "Congruence" today.

- ### *Presentation to many*

This is a development of the existing Skills. Thinking of the situation of the buyer and how he may not be the sole decision maker may well mean that the salesman now has to present himself, his company, his products, his services and the features, advantages and benefits of doing business with him to a group of interested parties. We do not propose to describe a presentation skills course here but if good empathy and sensitivity have been achieved with the buyer, the salesman may have some insight into the characters to whom he is presenting. A good relationship with the main buyer may yield information about what each of the decision makers has as a key driver or motivation in the purchase. It is this understanding that can make all the difference.

- ### *Negotiation*

This would form part of interpersonal or communication Skills. Again we do not propose to write a negotiations skills programme right here but it is worth noting that this situation is more likely to require some flexibility than the earlier FMCG example. Flexibility may mean looking at variety in products, costs, after sales service, delivery times or some of the terms and conditions attached to the purchase. This means some negotiation is required and as such it is fundamental for the salesman to know what range of options is in his gift to negotiate upon and what are the acceptable (profitable?) limits to his negotiations? Interestingly it may lead to internal negotiations within the selling organisation and it may not be the salesman who is the final arbiter, but he will need to have all his facts and figures, and those of his client available to bring to the negotiating table.

•   *Selling to Groups*

Building upon the group presentation and possibly some negotiation, it is important to realise that whilst the buyer may be the one who will sign any contract he is not the sole purchaser. Each person who has an interest in the decision will need to be won over, although it may be that some have less sway than others in the ultimate decision. Using any knowledge built through the empathy and sensitivity to the buyer's situation can prove invaluable here. It is important for the salesman to realise the motivations and "angles" of each person who has a part in what we may refer to as a decision making unit. This is possibly overarching and covers all the skills needed to address one buyer but introduces the skills of balancing one to many rather than one to one.

•   *Maintaining, sustaining and developing relationships*

With all that we have said it is probably emerging that this will not result in an instant sale. Also, the nature of the product and goods in the example here suggest the possibility of subsequent sales. There is also the perennial possibility that the company may move to new premises, make an acquisition, expand or in some way need more of your product and service. The relationship is not only with the buyer as we have seen there are a number of vested interests here. The art is to weave a relationship with all people involved at an appropriate level of relationship. The buyer is the principal relationship and should be maintained as such but having some connection with the users and other decision makers is valuable. Understanding the buyer and not "treading on his toes" will be critical. This is likened to the behaviour of perseverance and probably couples with interpersonal skills.

Knowledge

We have suggested that some additional areas of important Knowledge have emerged in this new context. The original Knowledge elements have not really changed and for the sake of completeness, but with no further elaboration, let's list them here:

- *Product Knowledge*

- *Competitors Products*

- *Market Knowledge*

The new elements are:

- *Political awareness*

It may be useful to say we mean politics with a small 'p' here. We are not expecting an in-depth Knowledge of political systems and characters. Rather we are talking about being aware of the "who is who" in the buying decision. Beyond that it includes some understanding of the structure of the organisation and where the "power" lies within the group to whom you are selling and presenting.

It is about understanding the clients' buying and decision making processes. It is also about understanding what information they need, who the influencers are, what timescales they are working to and any constraints that may exist and who reports to whom!

- *Identifying needs and the "political levers"*

This builds directly from the political awareness we just discussed and may be seen to be part of the same thing. Needs are interesting in themselves as we easily feel we have established the need for (in this case) office furniture of a particular type and style. However the need is deeper than that and may be over-lain with budgetary requirements, hierarchical and or social parameters deriving from the organisation's culture and the concepts of value for money, longevity, functionality, fitness for purpose and so on. Being aware of these and where the "political levers" or drivers are can make a huge difference between success and failure in the sale.

Reflections

Is this more of the same or different? In the Far East they have an expression which they express in English and which says "Same, same but different". What a great expression as it sums up so much of life. We have seen that so much of the experience in the FMCG example and in the era of consolidation still apply in the era of expansion and the capital goods context. There have been one or two tweaks to some areas of Behaviours, Attitudes, Skills and Knowledge and some new ideas were introduced too.

Part of what we need to do is understand why this is important. If we don't see the importance of it all we will find short-cuts and ways of avoiding doing some of the things inherent in this process. Some of them may feel difficult or alien and certainly they may require some Behavioural change.

The interesting thing is that often we just do a job without thinking about how it works or what we are trying to achieve. What we are doing here is helping to focus on the elements that we have seen make the difference between good and great salesmen. It has also been our experience that those who absorb tips, ideas, concepts and Knowledge from a wide range of sources and then apply them in their context and with their personality usually outshine the rest. Yes, there are the 'naturally gifted' but many of them will find sources of inspiration, challenge and insight too.

One of the key things that changed in our example here is that we are now concerned with selling to more than one person and have several people to influence, persuade, win over and get to buy a product and service. This impacts Behaviours, Skills and to an extent Knowledge too. At the Behavioural level we mentioned patience, persistence and consistency. We could perhaps put the first two as Attitudes too. The key though is that that urgency that was so prevalent in the era of expansion and which still exists today needs to be controlled. Perhaps the homily here can be taken from the story of the hare and the tortoise. To sell in that kind of environment and many others those Behaviours were and are essential. Some may see this as being more akin to "account management" than selling but bear in mind someone still needs to close a sale here!

Perhaps the most fundamental difference that drives this need for Behavioural change (or awareness at least) is that it is a longer cycle sale with more than one person involved. This emphasises the need for building relationships; multiple relationships. This is Behavioural, perhaps attitudinal, certainly demands skill and benefits from Knowledge.

Selling into organisations requires us to know that inside an organisation there are many different groups and group relationships or "dynamics" going on. What is also interesting is that when these seemingly disparate groups are "confronted" by something which is outside the organisation, they bind together and find their commonality. Put simply it's a process about what we may call in-groups and out-groups. The out-group is the salesman and the organisation he represents and the in-group is the new found unity of all the internal groups within the buying organisation.

It is not in the salesman's best interest to try and fragment the in-group nor to try and win against it. The relationship piece and understanding the individual or team needs gives the opportunity to the salesman to allow the buying organisation to remain united whilst giving all the individuals the necessary information and decision making opportunities.

This may seem a perverse way of working but it is important to allow an organisation to present its united front to the outside world, whilst it may argue and debate internally to come to the agreed decision. We have all seen organisations from the small family unit to national governments descend into public displays of in-fighting. This has so many ramifications but for the sales person it may have some particular significant effects. It will inevitably slow the whole process down, it is likely to cast the salesman in the role of "baddie", the one who caused the rift (even though all he may have done is cause the existing rift to become evident). Worse still, it may drive the buying organisation to another salesman or selling organisation.

There are a number of people involved in deciding whether to buy or not and whether to buy from *you* or not. We have found it risky at best to forge just one strong relationship in an organisation anyway, but this example really emphasises the need to build multiple relationships. It is not possible here to describe every relationship you may need, nor the level to which it should be formed, but consider who is your main contact. The buyer is the first and fundamental "gate keeper" to the organisation and is ultimately the one who will sign your contract (or not). Being aware of his position and sensitive to his needs, pressures and constraints will help you enormously as a salesman. Ultimately the decision may rest with a CEO, CFO or even a committee but it is advisable not to alienate the buyer by going round him, over him or through him. Build that relationship solidly enough and you will get messages to the others or better still have access to them.

We have seen some organisations create multiple to multiple relationships where the CEO's, CFO's and others also get involved in the relationship. This can work well but adds to the complexity and requires some level of management by the key salesman. Our thought on that is use caution and discretion in building relationships. You may need the help of your own CEO or CFO to convince a client but building a matrix of relationships may not be as productive as the salesman building suitable relationships himself. The fundamental though is to realise that there are many relationships (well certainly more than one) to build successfully and that they need to be sustained and nourished.

By building the key relationship with the buyer on firm foundations, you may well have a better access to the knowledge and awareness you need. What are the budgetary constraints? Who else is involved in the tender process (who are your competitors in other words... if any)? Who are the key decision makers? What is the decision making process? What are the timescales? You may even get an insight into the "politics" of who are the key influencers, who has an axe to grind, whose department is being furnished, what are the hierarchies involved here and so on and so forth.

The in group / out group thoughts are not in the mind of anyone when entering the initial phases of a sale, and they may not always become apparent ; after all there is a huge number of cohesive, friendly and successful organisations. However, the sensitivity to be able to manage the relationship with a group and the individuals within it may well be fundamental to success and could well be a point of difference between competing selling organisations.

We cannot emphasise enough the importance and significance of relationship building in this whole enterprise.

Patience is a virtue in this entire process too. We know that many salesmen have a real sense of urgency and competitiveness and the idea is to win business and win it quickly. We have found that the pace of decision making in organisations, particularly in the public sector, is slower and needs to take due process and due diligence into the whole cycle. We described the longer cycle sale in this instance. Consider the situation; these are capital goods which will be a large expense very often. O.K. the costs can be dissipated or amortised over a period of years but whatever the financial treatment of the purchase it is likely to have an impact upon cash-flow. Some organisations may be confident enough to seek a sort of lease-purchase or full on hire scheme. Confidence comes from being large enough and secure enough to request such a deal and / or emotionally secure enough to avoid the rather "masculine" trait of the need to buy now, out right and for cash!

Here again we come back to the notion of joint buying decisions and the salesman's awareness and appreciation of the situation. Knowledge of the customer can be critical in this respect and knowing how they may need to finance a purchase can be useful. Here the individual approach may win over. Discussing finance options in the public arena of a large meeting may not win prizes or plaudits, but suggesting there may be financial options and discussing them separately with the finance representatives or your finance guys and the buyer's finance guys may well work better.

That there is a group of people involved in the purchasing process and decision process means that the salesman has to present to a group rather than the cosy chat in the stock room that we saw in the FMCG example. Presenting to groups requires a whole set of Skills and Behaviours but we do not intend to run a presentation skills programme here. Suffice to say that all people need to be engaged and this requires relevance, interest, eye contact and awareness of who they are and what their particular interest in the matter is. The formality or otherwise will be determined by the client and you may get an insight into this from the buyer.

It will help if you understand the buyer's relationship with others in the room. This is part of the political awareness of who is who and the relationships, hierarchy, protocols, authority and internal structures of the organisation. To the experienced this seems second nature like a master chef producing his signature dish; but to the novice or sous chef copying the master the ingredients let alone the recipe and cooking process may seem daunting. Trust that you can do it, imperfectly at first may be, but try and practise and things will come right! Especially if you have a good mentor or coach!

This aspect may be interpreted as the "political awareness" that we referred to before. Political awareness covers a multitude of aspects. It is the stuff about knowing who the decision makers are and who is responsible or reporting to whom. It is also knowing about the decision making process and what elements are important in a decision; if the decision is purely financial or if it is about practicality and functionality, the influences and the influencers may be different. In essence it all boils down to relationships again, but with the insight and benefit of knowing what relationships have the influence and in what way you might ensure you or your organisation can meet the requirements.

Relationship, sensitivity and awareness of who is who within the team you are selling to can be a distinct advantage. Likewise, sensitivity of how to deal with the approach to competitor knowledge can be advantageous. We need to be cautious against an attack on competitor's products and we should hold to that. Buyers may have many different outlooks on this aspect and it is true that they may turn to you for help in that minefield of understanding difference. However they may also perceive the salesman as arrogant and pushy if his Attitude is "Ours is the best and here are the reasons why...." Worse still would be if the salesman projects or states an Attitude that says "You'd be foolish to buy anything other than our product!"

This is all bound up in a set of curious things that we can bundle as morals, values, pride and self esteem or image. If this is a long cycle sale then you may well as salesman have the chance to understand your buyer well. Few of us wish to be pushed into a sale and few of us appreciate being told what to do. The era of expansion was the time in which that sense of independence and uniqueness became more apparent and we learned not to be too pushy. In the public sector buyers are protecting the public purse and may be more conservative (small 'c') or cautious in their decision making. Decisions will be bound by a high set of morals and values in many cases. This may be equally so in the private sector though sometimes less obvious when commercial pressures are brought to bear. However in either case the individuals concerned deserve and usually expect to be treated with respect, acknowledging their intelligence and expertise. An understanding again of who fits where in the decision process is important but a salesman should never lose sight of the purchasing manager, project manager or whoever brought them in. This relationship will endure and in spite of any internal differences within the buying organisation the salesman is well advised to remember who the gate keeper is.

On that point, trivial as it may seem, where a salesman is selling to an organisation it is worth considering the relationship with receptionists, security staff and personal assistants to the buying "team". These each deserve respect too and as an outsider one is never aware of the influence that they may bring to bear. A wrong word here or there can come back to haunt the salesman.

Much of this may seem obvious or common sense but sadly common sense is not as common as people think. We have learnt it from both sides of the buying and selling "fence" and we have seen and *made* some of these errors. There is no need to be sycophantic or ingratiating, but politeness, sensitivity, awareness and patience are useful traits to explore.

Knowing that competitors may also be involved in the tender process means all the more that the salesman needs to understand his own AND the competitor products. Even knowing that one's own is the superior product does not guarantee the sale as there are other factors in the sale that impact upon the ultimate decision.

That said it is still fundamental to know your own products inside out and to have a good appreciation of the differences between yours and your competitors'. It is not for us to enter ethical arguments here, but it was probably during this time, the era of expansion, that much of U.S. advertising started to draw comparisons between products; praising one's own and finding fault with the competitor.

By knowing our own products well we can point out the significance of how it meets requirements without referring to the competitor. In doing this we can also "educate" our customer in which areas to look at the competitor product...ultimately the comparison and decision must be theirs.

Bearing in mind there are a few people involved in this decision, it is important to give them all the information that is relevant to them. It is important to consider that the political awareness couples with this; who needs to know what? Why is that relevant to them? How might that compare with a competitor? So, which aspects do we wish or need to draw their attention to so that they might ask the right questions of others in a competitive quote situation? It is equally important to listen to feedback and questions coming from the buyer and his colleagues. With this there is often the temptation to fabricate a positive answer; if one does not exist or it is something you need to refer back to others in your organisation, be honest. (O.K., so we said we would not discuss ethics, but it is just a point of view....that has worked!) As the user or functional head of the team of users I may have a different perspective from the finance guy; the salesman cannot resolve all those internal debates and positions, merely supply good information designed to help each come to a good conclusion. It may mean some compromise within the client's organisation or between the supplier and the client.

As we continue the progression to the latest learning we have implemented in our sales process we need to confirm that what we are passing along the way has been useful.

In the era of expansion we saw a lot of change. People were finding more independence and were less bound by rules and regulations. This freedom, as it were, made differences for our sales approach as people began to feel more opportunity for choice.

Politically it was the era of greater individualism and opportunity which translated to all walks of life. Whilst within an organisation one conformed to its values and norms of Behaviour and Attitudes there was probably a greater assertiveness of "self" coming through. Clearly this was not universal at the time but it marked the trend towards a greater individualism.

It is interesting that our sales example was more about selling to a group rather than the individual then. However it is relevant because it serves to emphasise the importance of treating the team as a team but also as individuals. Relationships have always been important in selling but here we emphasise just how important they are. We have deepened the understanding of the value of respect for the individual to whom we are selling and those around him. We have started to explore a notion of trust in the salesman by the buyer too.

We have begun to explore the idea that as the salesman I may build great relationships but I am not on the inside of the buying decision (the in-group concept) and that my position is one of influence by providing timely and appropriate information upon which the buyers can make decisions.

We have also begun to look in a little more depth at product Knowledge and particularly competitor information. It is not necessary for us to "rubbish" the competitor but it is probably a sound idea to show our position of strength and invite the customer / buyer to explore the right questions to ask our competitors.

We have also begun to understand a little more of the complexity of pride, self esteem, values and morals as part of the backdrop to selling. These are likely to become recurrent themes especially for independent and more self-reliant buyers. A buyer will not want to be pushed into a decision and pride may mean the salesman has to act more tactfully and discreetly in tackling such issues as finance and payment.

No matter that this example was about selling to many, which added its own complexities, we still need to address the individuals involved as individual, unique human beings!

Much of selling is based upon respect and trust and it is clear that we should build these aspects into our selling manner as soon as we can. This is a major theme that we learned and emerges strongly in the present era of selling.

A summary

This was an era in which choice extended and customers began to assert a little authority and the salesman had to be more of a salesman. Selling oneself and one's product became more significant.

Focus in this era

In this era our focus and example was on Capital Goods being sold to a corporate buyer. This alone required changes in the key elements of selling as well as the progression we made in the era.

Motivation and Expectation

The buyer had a different view, often being like a "piggy in the middle" between the salesman and the organisation and individuals for whom he was buying.

Brand

Brand was growing up too with emphasis spreading from advertising and awareness to expectation and perception on the part of the customer. The earlier jingles had to have more meaning and carried a burden of expectation.

Key Elements of Selling

Some of these changed and some new ones were added but the basis of the previous elements remained.

Behaviours

The areas of Behaviour that were added or grew or changed were:

- Time management

As this became akin to account management, the salesman was looked upon as the one who would ensure that the entire selling organisation kept to time and time promises.

- Perseverance

An additional Behaviour was required as the sales cycle had extended. The salesman could not give up

- Consistency

With the extended sales cycle the salesman needed to remain consistent in what he said and did. Also if the sales organisation involves a variety of people they need to be consistent between themselves too.

Attitudes

The Attitudes may have been slightly tempered by the new expectations but what we find is that Attitudes generally remain throughout. Positivity

Skills

The initial Skills remained and generally were unaltered. However, given the nature of the new sales environment, we learned that some new Skills were essential.

- Empathy and Sensitivity

Primarily this is thought of in terms of the buyer but extends to all in the buying and selling process

Knowledge

The three main areas of Knowledge are perennial but given the new circumstance we saw a blend of Knowledge and Skills to allow success. The Knowledge aspects that were added in this time were:

- Political Awareness

Politics here is with a small "p" and covers the awareness of roles and involvement of the different individuals. It includes the Knowledge of who is responsible for what and what their "angle" may be!

Reflections

We completed the era by reflecting on how the above elements, expectations and brand all came together and the significance of each and their impact one upon another.

The Parable of Keith Murnane
as told by Barrie Smith

As a marine engineer Keith had travelled the world repairing engines in every ocean – and the Christmas prior to us first meeting had been the final straw. Wallowing in the engine room of a freight ship in the middle of the Indian Ocean for four days that included Christmas Day and Boxing Day had convinced Keith that there had to be an easier way of earning a living.

And so it was that Keith and I were in the office of Mr. Joe Attwood proprietor of J.P. Attwood Ltd in Stratford, East London a company with a large number of branches in the East End.

Keith had joined our company some eight months previously and had quickly established himself as a highly proficient sales person. So much so, that as I was about to take up my first management appointment he was promoted to take over my duties as a 'Major Accounts Executive Salesman' in London. I was in the process of introducing him to my, soon to be his, accounts.

Our company, Spillers Ltd. were an innovative marketing led company and we had just launched a whole new concept in branding. We were the manufacturers of quality canned pet foods and one of our most successful products was Topcat a fish based product that was highly successful both in sales volume for ourselves as the manufacturer and in terms of profit margin for the retailer. I would ask you, the reader, to remember Topcat was a FISH product.

Key to success in the competitive market we operated in were new products combined with in-store exposure or shelf space.

To meet these challenges we had launched two new varieties of Topcat, one being chicken based and the other of rabbit. They were launched in a pack of three tins, one of each variety at a very competitive price. Today varieties of well known brands of many products are the norm but the launch of varieties of Topcat was a first in the U.K.

It was this product that we were launching in the office of Mr. Attwood and Keith was conducting the sales meeting.

The norm was to secure the order for regularly stocked products and then to make the sale of new or promotional products - and everything was going well. The normal order was secured and Keith then presented this totally new concept in product launches.

Mr. Attwood listened carefully to the proposition and then spent time explaining to us that he felt this was almost unfair – what was unfair was that he was about to make a very healthy profit from the deal but it would mean increasing his range of pet food products, almost by default. The business proposition was too good to be ignored

However Mr. Attwood was not going to go quietly – he smiled at us and came out with his killer objection.

"How do you know cat's like Chicken or Rabbit?"

Keith smiled back, and delivered the best close I have ever observed.

"Mr Attwood – Have you ever seen a cat with a fishing rod?"

That was truly a moment of "Congruence" – and I remembered my lesson from Les March and said nothing at all.

THE ERA OF AMBITION

In which we see the changes in customer demand, attitude and behaviour and how that impacts upon the needs and skills of salespeople and in which the Behaviours, Attitudes, Skills and Knowledge of the sales person are developed to accommodate the aggressive customer attitudes of "I Want and I Will Have"

Background to the era

An interesting time when it was really about ambition and drive but which in hindsight was probably a time of desire, expectation and demand too. At the time people were not aware they were being avaricious but it was clear that they were driven to ownership, possession and an even greater freedom than had existed before. We may well refer to this era as a time when buyers, consumers, customers or clients had the attitude of "I want and I will". Interestingly, because of the drive for ownership some of the skills of the salesman went into decline. Perhaps this was an era where the shift of 'power' from salesman to buyer really became evident, but also the era in which the greatest salesmen still proved their worth and value!

This was an era that embraced the end of what many in the United Kingdom would refer to as the Thatcher years, so named after the first female Prime Minister of England, Mrs (later Lady) Margaret Thatcher. Thatcher's rise to such a position served to encourage women generally to believe in themselves more. This resulted in greater striving for gender equality, independence and shared decision making in many homes. It was less of a time of men dominating the work environment and women being homemakers or housewives. This was a fundamental social change and in many cases shifted the emphasis in decision making in the home.

It was the era when State owned monopolies, telephones and power for example, became publically owned organisations and individuals were encouraged to become share holders in those organisations. Also Mutual Societies, strictly speaking non profit making organisations that ploughed money back into the business for the benefit of all. Many were financial institutions such as Building Societies, the main mortgage lenders. If you had a mortgage or a savings deposit with these organisations when they became public you automatically became a share holder.

Thus the shift in Britain was quite dramatic. Polit0ically, economically and socially many things were changing. People living in "social" or local government owned housing were given the chance to become owners of their property. This was a huge cultural shift and brought many more people into ownership. Property and share ownership were no longer the preserve of the so called middle and upper classes. Conservatism was attempting to equalise society. Very interesting times indeed. The legacy of the Thatcher era and her successors was a time perhaps summed up by the world-renowned music group Queen 'I want it all and I want it now'! It certainly had that feel with house prices soaring and money easy to borrow. People were committed, perhaps *over* committed to a great lifestyle and their personal ambition. It was not unusual for families to take two or three holidays abroad in this time. As we suggested before, selling had become almost order taking, but good sales people still maintained an edge.

So what else was happening in this era of ambition? Well firstly we need to remind ourselves that it is not totally synonymous with the Thatcher years and all that they brought. There is an overlap but this era was as much a legacy of the Thatcher years as it was part of it. It was an era of technological expansion and lifestyles were changing to accommodate more technology in the workplace and in the home. For example the now ordinary www or html or http initials were only in their infancy as the Internet became available to the public and expanded rapidly to the turn of the century. It was also the time when games like the Play Station first started to appear in homes. Mobile phones became ubiquitous and smaller in size, with longer lasting inbuilt, rechargeable batteries.

Businesses were now able to keep in touch with employees almost constantly and reports after meetings away from the office were almost instant. The pace of life moved on a notch or two.

The world became a smaller place with internet connections but also at last the rail link between Europe and England was opened with the first transport running through the Channel Tunnel. The connections with space were continued with Shuttle flights but also the launch of the Hubble Telescope. For some this heralded new freedoms and looking beyond here and now. It was a time for other freedoms with Nelson Mandela being released from jail in South Africa and Poland having its first president in Lech Walesa. Also the USSR fragmented into the original states and countries. But it was sadly a time when war still continued and the Middle East was a place of angst. With Desert Storm raging in Iraq there were tensions in and amongst Middle Eastern Countries. It is supposed that this also brought an attack into New York at the World Trade Centre that later suffered a fatal attack.

With so many things happening it was hard to keep track of the events except that TV had moved on and there was a greater level of news broadcasting which included sad events like Royal divorces and the death of Princess Diana. The latter event had a profound effect upon Britain which seemed as a nation to be shocked and in genuine mourning.

Slightly cheerier examples included scientists cloning a sheep (Dolly) and a Tiger (Woods) winning a first major golf event. Musically the western world was treated to the Macarena with its formulaic dance moves. It was also a time when "Girl Power" came in the form of the Spice Girls whose hits included Wannabe. Elton John's Candle in the Wind was revived in a new guise for the funeral of Princess Diana and Billy Ray Cyrus sung about his Achy, Breaky Heart. R.E.M. continued their success with songs including Losing my Religion. And, just to prove how free the society had become the song, Let's Talk About Sex Baby was released by Salt N Pepa.

Freedom, no real financial worries, a carefree attitude to money and ownership then typified the era of ambition. Buyers were in the ascendant but selling was still a valuable art, especially in encouraging buyers to buy specific products or services or to choose specific brands. The market was almost awash with "me too" products and the good salesman was attracting buyers to his products and services.

Focus in this era

Our focus here is more about selling Financial Services to individuals or family groups (itself an education as to who "wears the trousers" to use a rather dated expression) and selling a product that wasn't always perceived as important. Success and repeat business depended upon integrity and being ethical....selling what a customer needed and could afford.

This was challenging in an era where the customer's focus was on wants more than needs. This drove some new ideas and skills for the salesman in order to be successful.

Expectations and Motivations

Our example in this section is a much more personalised selling and is based in Financial Services, primarily selling life insurance to customers whose attitude may well have been along the lines of "live now, pay later!" So this would not be an easy sale; insuring one's life was not a top priority for many people. So, whilst many sales skills were not needed as people were more assertive in buying, in Financial Services, especially pensions and life insurance, sales skills were possibly in the ascendancy!

It is sadly true that some salesmen were a bit too pushy and gained a bad reputation for the industry. It is a fine line sometimes between being scrupulous and fair and "pushing" for the sale. This is especially true where commissions play a large part of the salesman's compensation and benefits.

Motivation for many salesmen at the time was to take orders; for others it was to attract customers to their specific products; for others it was sell almost at any price and for others it was about building relationships and creating a loyal following. For customers it was about buying what they wanted, needed or felt they "deserved" or that which would show them in a good light and successful. For most, both salesmen and customers it was probably a time when the prime motivation was short term gain and pleasure with no real concept of long term security or well being.

Many were fortunate to be in organisational schemes for pensions, some had private health care as part of their salary package and the welfare state was there for any who fell on hard times. This meant the general motivation was to "live for today".

Brand

Brand was emerging more and more as a key to getting sales of a particular product. This had grown from the early days of advertising and had spawned a great and wealthy industry of advertising agencies, public relations experts and the emergence of a "web presence" which we will return to in the next era!

Brand as a word probably emerged from an activity that showed ownership; branding cattle by the cowboy in the United States. From those potentially humble beginnings, brand started to emerge as much more multifaceted and included emotions, character and personality within its spectrum.

The main purpose of brand was to help consumers distinguish between products and services. From the salesman's perspective it was about demonstrating what became known as the USP (Unique Sales Proposition). As marketers wrestled with brand they started to make their own USP and called it UVP (Unique Value Proposition).

Some differences were on price; some were on quality; some were on service and yet others were on a whole package of product and guarantees and support. Some brands appealed to lifestyles and followed the concept of "live for today" whilst others tried to buck the trend and show that there was some longevity and quality, preservation and personal welfare were worth investing in. Life insurance had to take that longer view as an industry but within the industry the USP's were on price as much as any other product or service. Quality and reliability as well as longevity were perhaps prerequisites in terms of the insurance company being straightforward and easy to deal with and paying out when claims were made.

Brand was much more than marketing or advertising campaigns and included what were affectionately known as the "5 P's" of marketing, namely: Price, Placement (distribution), Promotion, People and Product. It was probably in this era that we really became aware of the significance of people as a differentiator in the "style" in which we wanted 'our' organisation to be represented. A classic example was often quoted as Nordstrom, the US department store which gave exemplary personal service. Others were simpler at the time and included the McDonald's smile. There was a whole thing about brand with both and most of us have experienced McDonald's; if you get a chance to, do experience Nordstrom.

The key elements of selling

With the customers generally buying what they felt suited them, focussing attention on the short-term and marketing taking the high ground, selling in its purest form had to build upon all the skills that had emerged since the era of expansion. Salesmen had to represent their organisation and product or service; they had to negotiate with customers who were used to having things their own way and they needed to align the sale with the customer's needs, where probably the customer was only interested in wants and desires.

Selling was probably more about order taking in this era as customers had choice, to a large extent knew what they wanted, had money to spend and lived for the moment. The expression "money is burning a hole in your pocket" really did apply to many customers in this era of ambition.

However it was equally true that salesmen were trying to highlight differentials in order to attract people to buy from them rather than competitors and this clearly helped many to develop Skills and Knowledge. In some cases salesmen also adapted and developed Behaviours and accentuated Attitudes that were attractive to customers.

In promoting products and services in financial services that were not top of mind for customers, salesmen had to develop and ensure that they worked on things that would create the alignment we mentioned before.

Behaviour

It is important to recognise that the behaviours we discussed in earlier eras did not suddenly become redundant. Increasing use of technology allowed a remote salesman to maintain contact with his office and keep his manager informed on a daily or weekly basis of the activity he was undertaking. However the basics of recording, reporting, time management, reliability and preparation were still fundamental. With this emergence of more technology, recording and reporting may have been more instant and easier to perform but they demanded different actions from individuals whilst the Behaviour of "doing" them remained very important if success was to be achieved.

Those behaviours learnt in selling to many and over a long cycle remained relevant as often these were sales that took more than one 'bite of the cherry' to complete and may involve more than one decision maker. So perseverance, patience and consistency were still significant behaviours to manage and foster for the salesman.

With social, political, financial and ownership changes going on it was important that "new" behaviours were included. They require some interactivity and are built upon open minded attitudes.

These "new" Behaviours were predominantly captured as two elements although they probably encompassed more:

* *Increased awareness*

The Behavioural aspect of this was being aware of the fact that customers' positions and attitudes were changing. Being aware of this meant that the salesman could not be complacent, or if he was he became an order taker. Being aware that customers would choose and often would buy things because they could, would lead to a successful salesman building new skills as well as we will see below.

His Behaviour had to "accept" the position that many customers adopted was that of buyer rather than someone who could be easily sold to. Customers were often dismissive and may have appeared in this era to be arrogant towards salesmen.

The behaviour was part of a shift in the "control" of the sales transaction. Those who were incapable or simply chose to ignore this would themselves be ignored. Clearly this behaviour was a development of the existing awareness that successful salesmen were displaying.

+ *Availability to customers*

With society becoming a twenty four hours a day, seven days a week culture the smart organisations were making themselves available to their customers on a similar basis. Smaller organisations would have struggled to achieve this but even medium sized organisations started to set up call centres which have migrated to contact centres over time. Some were not able to offer a twenty four hour service but tried to have an extended hours' presence and like retail establishments started to "trade" on each of the seven days in the week. For some individual salesmen this meant that they had to extend their working day and be available at times that the customer expected rather than traditional nine till five.

For our financial services salesman this certainly meant evening and weekend work to be available when the customer had time. It would be normal too for this type of transaction to take place in the customer's own home. So perhaps the behaviour of flexibility was also fundamentally important to the successful salesman.

Clearly in this era the customer was more independent and more demanding than before and the salesman had to adapt to survive.

Attitudes

We have already described how Behaviours had to remain constant as well as developing in new ways over time. Attitudes may be seen as more fixed and therefore less adaptable to change. That infers an important attitude within itself. For salesmen to be successful they had to be open minded, adaptable and prepared to follow or instil change. All of the personal attitudes we came across earlier in the eras of consolidation and expansion remained important in the era of ambition. In fact perhaps a salesman's ambition had been one of his driving forces and attitudes all the way through and whilst this remained important, the wise salesmen would not confront a customer's ambition with his own.

This openness and sensitivity was fundamental to continued success. Confrontation in a market place where the customer was beginning to "flex his muscles" would have been counterproductive.

Additional to the attitudes we already discussed, in the era of ambition it became important to recognise and act upon some "new" Attitudes. These were probably present in good salesmen all along but really emerged in their own right at this time.

- *Increased customer sensitivity*

This Attitude was possibly the most important in this potentially conflictual environment. Salesmen always have needed an Attitude that addresses the "value" of the customer even if the belief is not always that the 'Customer is King.' The customer is the decision maker and awareness and sensitivity to their needs had to increase in this era to accommodate their options in choosing products and services.

The customer is the final arbiter of whether they will buy or not and it is important to recognise that fact. The salesman has the role of demonstrating how the item they are selling will meet the customer's needs or add value to his life. Especially where the customer was being more assertive of new found "purchasing power" it was important to be sensitive to this fact. However, successful salesmen had to pay attention to the next Attitude which emerges from this.

It was very common in the era of ambition to regard the customer as "King" and many organisations actually ran training programmes based upon this premise. We should neither debunk that notion nor criticise those that developed the programmes and the attitudes that drove them. Maybe it is the blessing of hindsight as we were probably involved in similar programmes ourselves, but the most successful salesmen were those who had a balanced view. Going overboard in believing and making the customer feel like a king could be patronising and could lead to 'allowing him to buy' something totally inappropriate. As we will see in the skill developments of the era in a moment, a productive Attitude was that the customer should be respected, but he possibly did not have the font of knowledge that the professional salesman possessed. In respect of that, good Product Knowledge and Competitor Knowledge remained as significant as ever. The craft, as we will shortly see, was the ability to treat the customer as king and yet ensure their awareness of what they were buying was enhanced so their decision was informed.

This was really the main feature of the final Attitude

- *Openness to customer's choice and sometimes fickleness*

It was important to recognise that customers may make odd and unexpected choices and may also display fickleness occasionally. The Attitude really was about acceptance of this fact and not to judge the customer's choice. Judging or feeling superior may lead to conflict or confrontation and ultimately there will only be one winner, the customer. This openness may not always result in a sale but it was part of the bigger Attitude that this is a long game and to win overall is better than creating tensions along the way!

Skills

As with Behaviours and Attitudes those mentioned in earlier eras were still relevant in the era of ambition but the backdrop to selling had changed as we have already observed. With customers' increasing awareness and independence ("I'll buy it because I can") the true salesman had to update and refine his Skills. There were some areas of new understanding that really emerged strongly at this time although they may have been operating already. Now they took on a tremendous significance of their own and changed the emphasis of the selling conversation.

These concepts remain significant today and do seem to demarcate between success and moderate selling ability. We have seen great differences emerge in sales performance as clients have developed these enhanced Skills. The important thing is to understand them and commit to them so they become the norm. Selling must still reflect the personality of the individual but with these Skills salesmen differentiate themselves.

• *Personality or Behaviour identification*

This probably overlaps with Knowledge but we also need to look at it as a skill. Customers were now more independent and thought more for themselves which meant that we needed to understand them and interact with them differently. The skill is in identifying "types" of personality and behaving towards them appropriately. As people we will only observe the behaviours of others but these often reflect the deeper characteristics or even the personality of an individual. Recognising one's own type or style of behaviour allows for an improved interpersonal relationship with customers, as well as colleagues, bosses, friends and family. So we see this as an extension or development of inter-personal skills.

There are many ways to describe and define the styles and types but generally they correspond to the predominant behaviours and attitudes of people. They can be detected through body language, the words spoken and the style, tone and pace in which they are spoken, proactivity, reactivity and people or task orientation. The classic proponents of the "social styles" are Wilson Learning[1] who proffer it as a way for colleagues to improve interrelations and therefore working performance. The underpinning concept of behavioural styles can help salesmen too and operate best in circumstances where the style is recognised and responded to. It can be a very quick process for people to "see" the styles in others and yet some, perhaps less perceptive may take time to be more accurate. However once the cues are understood they can be invaluable. Let's return to the style cues in the Knowledge section, but for now we will look at the skill element.

The Wilson Learning definitions suffice to be a good basis for us here. Those with a task and proactive orientation are drivers; people orientation and proactive are expressive; people orientation and reactive are amiable and finally task oriented reactive styles are referred to as analytical (See diagram below). In the sales context we may see people as being on a dimension of thinking and feeling (task or people oriented) and a second dimension of cautious to "calculated" risk takers (reactive to proactive). The skill comes in two forms: recognising the style and then responding to it appropriately or in such a way as to relate most successfully to that individual.

We are probably all familiar with the expression "he doesn't suffer fools gladly" which may be an aspect of driver behaviour. "He'd do anything for anybody" could be a description of an amiable while the "life and soul of the party" could be an expressive or "he's always got his nose in a book" could be an analytical. Those are very simplistic descriptions and may not always work, but hopefully serve to start showing the differences of style.

1 Wilson Learning can be found at http://www.wilsonlearning.com

By beginning to respond appropriately it would help the salesman to "get on the same wavelength" as the customer and start to establish that mysterious thing called rapport. Whether it is true rapport or not is moot but at least it is a start to communicating more appropriately and effectively. We will explore this further in a later section.

To begin with, where might you place yourself or people you know on the quadrant below?

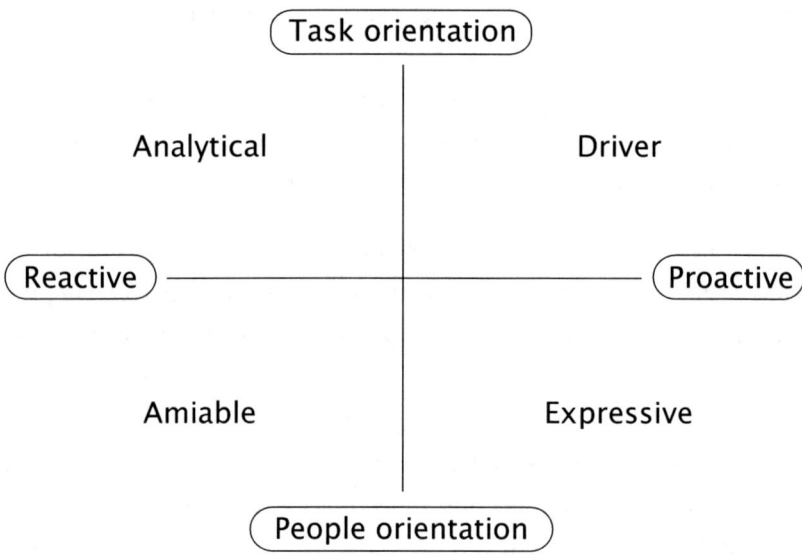

Approaching each "type" can only be based upon the behaviour they demonstrate. For example someone displaying analytical behaviour is likely to ask many technical or detailed questions and then reflect upon your answers. This reflection is probably a process of determining if your response matches what they may already believe (or know) or if your product or service matches their needs. It is not possible to push them through these stages rapidly as part of their "style" is to take time, analyse and think things through. An expressive person will possibly go through the stages faster and buy if he likes the product or service or you as the salesman. An amiable type is likely to be indecisive but give every indication they love everything until it comes to the crunch of a close. A driver may be in a rush, want minimum details but sufficient "evidence" to support his decision.

- *Open Questions*

Coupled with the understanding of type or style, but also very significant on its own was the notion of asking "open" questions. Most often we will refer to these as the "soft fact" questions. This is a strong development of the existing skill of questioning and listening.

Open questions help the salesman in helping the customer to become aware of his or her own attitudes towards something. It is interesting that whilst we may use hard factual information in the process of buying, most of our purchases are directly influenced by emotions or attitudes. What we believe, think or feel about something is going to have an impact upon our buying decisions.

You will recall *open questions* are those that begin with "what, where, when, why, how or who" and were immortalised by Kipling for whom they were 'the honest serving men who taught him all he knew'. From his poem "The Elephant's Child" the first few lines run....

> I KEEP six honest serving-men
> (They taught me all I knew);
> Their names are What and Why and When
> And How and Where and Who.

For the salesman they provide a great way to help understand, and help your customer understand their own beliefs, needs, wants and even emotional response to certain things, most notably the "thing" the salesman is trying to sell. We ask you to recall that this era was when consumers were living 'for now' and buying what they wanted when they wanted because they could. We also ask you to recall that our sales medium in this section is financial services including such products as life insurance.

In these circumstances it was important to help the customer realise the longer term benefits and the "responsibility" they had to others. Life insurance was easily dismissible by most people as the lifestyle was all about living for now and because of that there was no real sense of future or that others may be left bereft if the main breadwinner ceased to be inputting to the coffers. It was also one of those areas that made people feel uncomfortable or even squeamish as it made us face up to mortality. To a person in their twenties for example mortality seemed very remote and to be confronted with it by a salesman seemed inappropriate.

Armed with this awareness, the successful salesman used the open questions to help the potential client explore. It is true that some salesmen were more explicit and direct than others but it is equally true that those who had an understanding of people were very successful.

For example a direct approach might be "What would happen to your wife's lifestyle if you had died?" A more genteel approach may be "How would you feel about your wife having to manage without your income?"

Both confront the same issue and make the potential purchaser face up to his or her mortality.

The more sensitive approach and use of open questions would help the client review their attitudes and beliefs. Of course they would also look at the logical aspects of affordability, value for money and benefits, but these were often secondary to the consideration of whether the product had a place in their lives to start with.

It is impossible here to go through every open question that may be appropriate for every product or service in every situation. Suffice to say that we have seen great improvement in sales through using open questions in many different sectors of industry including travel, finance, health, communications and general retail.

The basis of the questions is to establish in the salesman's mind, and often in the customer's mind too, what is the reason for buying, how will the product or service be used, what value it will add to life and so on. It is a great way to explore the features a customer is really needing and wanting and to match an appropriate product and service to those features as an advantage and benefits.

This may well be the first time a customer has been asked such a question and therefore considered a belief or understanding that he may hold and may have held for a long time. The significance and impact of these questions can be immense.

Consider buying a car for example. There will be logical questions about usage, mileage, types of journey, number of passengers, child safety seat requirements and so on, but there will also be the attitudinal or emotive questions about colour, upholstery, performance, style and so on. The interesting thing is the debate over the logical and emotional decision, a point to which we will return. The facts are that many salesmen avoid or at least neglect the emotional or attitudinal side (the so called soft facts), often at the cost of a sale.

In some respects salesmen at this time were becoming aware of the reputation of some of them being "pushy". We'll explore this theme in the next era which is where we really came to understand it. The use of open questions is not pushy if used well and conversationally. Like all instances where questions are advised, the supportive aspect of attentive listening is essential. We have seen great use of open questions ruined by inattentiveness. For example, it might be like this in a holiday company:

> Agent: *What type of location are you looking for?*
>
> Customer: *On the beach or as close to it as possible*
>
> Agent: *What is the main thing you would like to do whilst away?*
>
> Customer: *Relax in the sun, on the beach, read and play in the water*
>
> Agent: *I have this fabulous two bedroom apartment in the town centre of Los Pallios, about ten minutes from the beach. How does that sound?*

We'll leave you to draw your own conclusions about how well it meets the requirements, but how would you feel as the customer? Had you been listened to?

The agent had done well with a couple of good exploratory open questions, but had not really matched the features of her property search to the customer's desires. Open questions *and* active listening have to be combined to be effective. This can allow a conversational (less pushy seeming) approach too.

◆ *Creating an opportunity bigger than the cost*

Some may see that this is not a skill but as it is teachable or learnable it is included here. A build upon the open question techniques as a precursor to a sale, another aspect of success is helping to create a sense that the opportunity or benefit of purchase is greater than the cost. By cost here we do not only mean financial cost but will include inconvenience, sacrifice of one thing for another or maybe time. There are other costs too but what we are seeking to do here is help the customer to see the opportunity is greater than the cost. This technique may often be used in handling objections, to which we will return later. It can also, possibly salvage the holiday agent's poor listening or poor matching in the example above. If for example other aspects of the apartment, nightlife and so on were important the opportunity (great apartment, close to the nightlife) may outweigh the cost (further from the beach).

Again it is important to listen and above all to have the whole story before making recommendations and trying to close a sale. Opportunities may not be seen as such unless we know the whole story, so plenty of open questions to establish real need and desires are a prerequisite to being able to make an opportunity seem bigger than the cost. Trying to recommend too early can often lead to an inappropriate suggestion and create more barriers and objections than reduce them

The estate agent who only hears "Three bedrooms" and doesn't bother to explore kitchen, garden, access and so on may be off down the recommendation of a second floor apartment whilst the customer has a "picture" of a cottage in mind. No amount of opportunity and cost relationship is likely to resolve that one.

Clearly the whole piece is important and only when all aspects of questions, listening and seeing opportunities can the next piece fall properly into place.

♦ *Presenting to needs and wants*

In this era we were aware that most purchases were based upon wants and here we had to help someone see a genuine need and benefit from a financial services purchase.

This part of the process really is just before the close of the sale where the salesman has listened carefully, helped the customer build their own attitude and response to what is important and then makes suitable recommendations. There may not always be the perfect fit so it may be that we, as salesmen acknowledge that and explore alternatives....This may mean going back to a couple more open questions and exploring the opportunity and cost paradigm.

• Handling objections

If we did get it wrong and customers raised objections, techniques had moved on and were probably more successful. They certainly were more empathetic with customers and the acronym ACE appeared, standing for Acknowledge, Clarify and Explain.

The ACE methodology worked thus:

The salesman would acknowledge the issue that the customer had with price or whatever the objection was. The form of words varied but was probably something like "That's interesting Mr X". Experience showed that the words "that's interesting" were probably the most likely to allow the salesman to stay neutral and non confrontational. Then the salesman would clarify what the issue or "problem" was with a form of words that played back to the customer the concerns he had expressed in the objection. It may have gone something like "From what you have told me Mr X, the issue seems to be a b c. Is that right?" This positioned the salesman as a kind of counsellor, and allows them to explain a solution that will enable the customer to take a different stance without losing face. "Let me explain....."

This approach in handling objections should be reserved for the really critical, decision influencing objections that may arise the sales process.

This could still be mildly confrontational and appear to accuse the customer of being wrong whilst the salesman was right. But it did acknowledge the customer and allow him to express his concerns, and as such was a development of how things had been before.

The aspect of selling of "creating" awareness then matching needs was always important but perhaps gained greater significance in the context that was emerging in the era of ambition, especially as buyers were buying in spite of themselves and in spite of salesmen.

Knowledge

All of the Knowledge areas we discussed in the earlier eras were still relevant in the era of ambition as they are today. However the context was different and the application of the Knowledge was probably different. The Skills, Attitudes and Behaviours in the way in which the Knowledge was delivered were all very important in the key to success and as ever the balance of all four areas was critical.

The relationship between Knowledge and Skill was very evident in the developed areas that we were using in the era of ambition. The skill of using open questions for example would only be useful when coupled with Product Knowledge, knowledge of what open questions are and knowledge of what information as a salesman we were trying to establish. In isolation the questions would have been great but would not have had practical value. Similarly the exploration of style or personality types had to have a basis in the Knowledge of typical characteristics of those styles.

+ *Personality style recognition*

Here we look at some of the characteristics which here are addressed as Knowledge. We have discussed, in outline the value of the skill of identifying behaviours in people so that as salesmen we can behave towards them appropriately and effectively.

We used the example of "not suffering fools gladly" as a possible characteristic of the so called driver style. In broader definitions we should say that this style is characterised by a desire to get things done and quickly. Movements and speech patterns tend to be quick and there is a sense of urgency so for a salesman to go into lengthy explanations and detail may well frustrate someone displaying this characteristic.

Describing the expressive character as the life and soul is an exaggeration for many of them but it indicates that they are generally able and willing to talk and be the lively presence in a conversation.

They are people focussed and tend to be a bit egotistical too. Like the driver they will be turned off by too much detail but talking to them about their emotional and attitudinal response to what you may be selling is likely to appeal. Likewise they like to talk about family and close friends and how things may appeal to them too.

As a salesman one of our greatest challenges is the amiable character who will agree with everything because they hate to offend, but then decline to buy because they don't like to commit and can be quite cautious. These are the ones who as often as not will "need to talk to the wife / partner/ significant other" or were "just enquiring". They can be sold to but we always recommend that they are not pushed as they can turn on you a bit like a cornered wild animal. Our experience has shown that the earlier we can engage an individual who displays amiable characteristics and get their contribution and involvement, the more likely we are to be successful.

Finally we have our analytical type of behaviour. Those that are characterised in this way are very likely to be the ones who ask detailed questions, may have already done their homework and know something of the product already. They love detail and facts and figures and that will often help them in a decision, although they too tend to be cautious in decision making, seeking all the facts (and probably making loads of comparisons) before they commit.

These basic outlines of possible customer characteristics and behaviours do not cover every aspect but give a clue. It is an important part, particularly in a complex sale of knowing which buttons to press to meet their needs, massage their egos or avoid wasting their (and your) time.

• Open Questions

I must emphasise that it is not possible to give every question for every situation, but knowledge of what they are and how they may work is invaluable.

The basic Knowledge is an understanding of the six opening words and truly understanding the value of asking them. Their use certainly helps to elicit more from the individual, their feelings, attitudes and motivations. Another useful piece of knowledge about them is how to use them most effectively with the different personality behaviours. Asking lots of open questions about feelings to a driver type will be at best counterproductive and at worst could set up confrontation. That is the last thing that a salesman needs. But even with the driver a couple of judicious open questions are very valuable. We find that in some circumstances we refer to these as "soft fact questions" as they are designed to elicit feelings, opinions and information that help the customer end up with the right product or service. They are "soft" because they are generally about attitude and opinion, whilst "hard facts" are the indisputable things such as date of birth, address and so on which may well be necessary in some sales situations (but not all). We have found it important to get the "hard fact" questions done and out of the way first so we can then focus on the "soft fact", attitudinal open questions and help the customer build the picture in his mind.

Undoubtedly the ability to ask effective soft fact questions makes almost a disproportionate difference to the success of a professional salesman.

We need to be cautious of using these questions to lead a customer too far in a direction they do not want to go. This can turn a good open question to a leading question. For example "What type of material do you prefer?" is an open question designed to make the customer think and can be followed by other open questions such as "Why do you prefer that?" or "What is about that material that attracts you?".

A leading question could start with one of Kipling's "six honest men" but is designed to get an answer that the salesman wants or needs. In the same circumstances a leading question may assume a particular material (the one that yields most margin, is the only one we have to sell or is simply the most popular). "What do you like about wool?" or "Why do you think wool would be suitable for your suit?" are both leading questions and have made assumptions about the customer's needs, wants or desires. They may be great as supplementary questions but we must be open and allow the customer to express an unfettered opinion first.

We have also experienced people asking a question totally out of context driven usually by the fact that the salesman has not listened effectively to what his customer is saying. We refer to these as *custard questions* as what relevance has custard to what the customer is saying? These non sequitirs can all too easily destroy the mood and the emotive elements we have helped the customer to build.

+ *Developing a network*

One aspect that is less clearly categorised in BASK terms is that of building and "using" a network. It may be an interpersonal skill and that is why it is included in this section.

Another key to success that emerged during the era of ambition was the use of referrals and the emergence networking. Selling to individuals, and often in their own homes it was critical for a salesman to establish a process whereby his clients would and could provide the next client and the next. This meant that quality had to be prevalent in the sense of personal reputation and the appropriateness of products and services sold. Personal reputation and recommendation had always been important but in this era, with a wider choice of products and services available it became more important to be recommended. Sadly this may not always have been the impression created and as an industry there was often a public jaundiced view that the products and salesmen were not all they should have been. Some of this will have been because of the reluctance of customers to confront the situations that the life insurance salesman "made" them face up to and also partly due to the culture of living for now and spending on what we want now, forget about the future.

• *Prospecting*

This is one area of sales that perennially brings many opinions and often concerns raised by both salesmen and customers is referred to as "cold calling". Some examples may include those we just explored in presenting "our" product and the Electro Company and Gas Corp. Many successful salesmen never cold call; some use their network and make a "warm" call; some send literature in advance so they have some means of introduction ("I sent our brochure last week. Did you receive it?"). Others have no problem in picking up the phone or calling in to see people and there are those who believe a brochure should only go to those who have expressed an interest in buying.

The attitudes of the salesman come to the fore here. Those aspects of perseverance, hunger and what we call "divine discontent" help to give the cold call shape and the salesman confidence. There is a potential downside that the confidence is overridden by a "macho" or even aggressive approach which is clearly counter productive. We are not suggesting a big dose of humility but we do urge sensitivity as often the cold call is an intrusion upon someone and can easily cause resentment and barrier building. Being aware of this, and, at the same time realising you have to establish fairly quickly the benefit to your potential customer of talking with you are critical elements of successful cold calling. This form of prospecting often fails because the sales person, in the desire to put everything to the prospect in the first few seconds of the call, is regarded by the prospect as "pushy" and even aggressive.

That's where the sensitivity helps. Think about the time of the call; think about what the customer may be doing (typing a report or preparing a meal or bathing the kids for example) and think about what may be beneficial to them.

So, how can you approach a cold call with sensitivity? With the sensitivity must come confidence or else the call will never happen. The confidence comes from the belief that your product or service is really good, has the potential to be useful for the customer and add value in some way to their life. The experience from the financial services world would be to use the cold call merely as a brief introduction, selling the "sizzle". By that we mean hearing and smelling the bacon in the pan enhances our desire to eat the bacon. In other words this is about making the product or service appealing and overcoming the sometimes personal objection that as the salesman you were "intruding". From that you would set a date in the diary for a fuller follow up meeting.

• *Knowing your numbers and ratios*

Recognising that we will not be successful 100 per cent of the time leads us to another concept of good selling; "know your numbers" or "know your ratios". In selling we are often using questions to help us filter or funnel down to find suitable products to offer to the customer. Selling overall is a funnelling or filtering process. Some of the filtering is an action by the salesman but also a lot of it is "self selection" by the customer. The numbers or ratios we are talking about here are those that relate to the customers we have contacted through to the sales and revenues we have made. Generally we can improve those ratios with experience and improved Skills but there comes a point when the ratios tend to plateau. That they plateau is not an excuse to stop making the effort and assume that everything will continue to flow....if we as salesmen rely upon the ratios to drive sales we will stop selling. The value of them is to keep us going *and* to try and improve them.

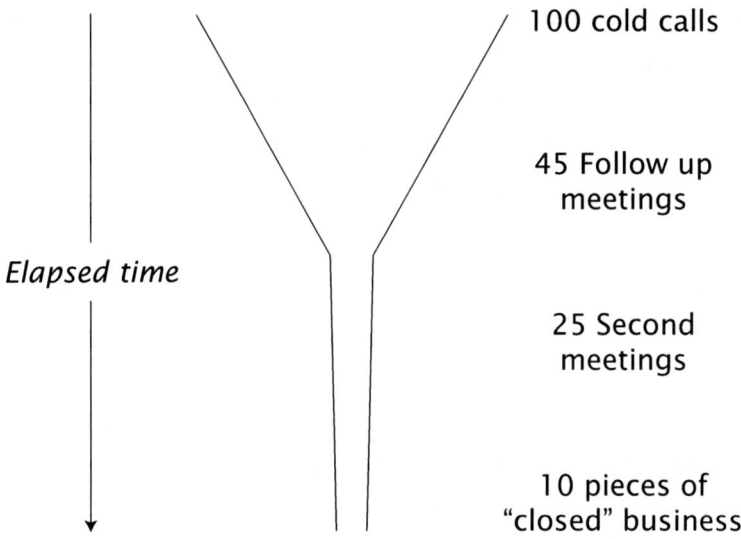

Elapsed time

100 cold calls

45 Follow up
meetings

25 Second
meetings

10 pieces of
"closed" business

We have added in "elapsed" time onto the diagram to illustrate that this does not happen in an instant and may vary considerably (as may the ratios) according to the sales environment, product or service. The measures may vary too with, for example retail environments measuring footfall rather than cold calls, others may measure enquiries to sales or whatever is most appropriate. Ours is merely an example of how we can have a guide to how well we are doing relative to our "norms".

Using these figures can be very important both to the manager and the salesman because, by understanding the sales ratios of both the salesman and the team the individual whether the manager or the salesman can manage activity. It is true to say despite many efforts, no manager or salesman has ever been able to manage results. We set out below a simple activity record. In this we see that our salesman has made fifteen approaches and successfully made ten appointments. Two of these appointments, for whatever reason were not kept. However, in the eight kept appointments our salesman made six presentations and achieved two sales. It follows that if our salesman wants to make four sales to achieve his target it is highly probable that he will have to make thirty approaches and it is that activity that he has to manage. Inevitably the longer these figures are maintained the more accurately our salesman will be able to forecast his results.

These figures will also create opportunities to correct weaknesses. As an example if our salesman improved his presentation skills and increased his sales achieved figure from 33.3% to 50% of presentations made his ability to achieve target would be enhanced and his need for a high level of approaches could be diminished. By using ratios in this way the salesman will have the motivation of knowing that he can define his own success, improve his sales skills and manage his future.

Approaches	Appointments Booked	Appointments Kept	Presentations Made	Sales Achieved
15	10	8	6	2

Reflections

We could be forgiven for thinking that 'selling is selling and it never really changes' but we would be wrong and doing a disservice to our profession. As the world has changed and customers' needs and perspectives have changed so selling has had to be flexible and adaptable to meet these new challenges.

We have tried to demonstrate that there are constant aspects of selling that endure no matter what but we have also tried to show the parts of modern selling that have emerged over the years. We have also put them into the context of the era in which they emerged as important and we know that in eras to come new things will emerge and some of the "traditional" methods may change again or even be replaced.

So what happened in the era of ambition that added to our repertoire and made new demands upon us and why are they important still? Most of it relates to the changing aspect of customer "Behaviour" driven by the ability to have more of what they wanted and to have it when they wanted it. That seemed to develop an almost careless attitude to buying that could be described as "well it doesn't matter if I don't like it or it's no good. I'll just get a replacement". That wasn't perhaps true of everything nor for everybody but it did throw down two main possibilities for the salesman. Firstly it afforded the opportunity to be an order taker and secondly the opportunity to hone professionalism, stand out from the crowd and get people to buy. In the second case the idea was to persuade people to buy from "me" because my product or service is best, but more importantly I have found your true needs and wants, helped you explore what they are for yourself and then I have matched my offering to your needs and wants.

The truth we have discovered is that many people will say "I was doing a lot of that anyway" and yet when we expose them to some of the key concepts learned in this era we discover they were not really using these techniques at all. Sadly the truth was and is that many sales people fall in to one of two camps: "let them buy" and "I have a green one so I'll push green ones". The former are really the order takers by another name, not making any real effort to promote or sell their product or service; rather they hope the customer will choose and buy from them. The latter make an effort but often it is misguided and difficult to do. It is a style which may be seen as confrontational and certainly one that results in lots of rejection and "no thanks" objections.

We discussed the notion of the customer being king and although they may not always receive regal service, it is true that the customer is the ultimate arbiter of whether they buy or not. Our emphasis has therefore been on finding the customer's real need and wants, their reason to buy and then showing how the opportunity represented by our product or service meets those needs and is greater than any cost either financially or in time, effort or other "sacrifice".

We have mentioned the attitudes and emotional responses that a person has about what they are buying are critical. Of course there is logical stuff involved in the decision making but it is interesting to note how much the emotional aspect has an influence upon choices. If we take life insurance as an example, there is the logic of affordable premiums and the amount a beneficiary would receive but the reason for buying it in the first place is more often than not based upon an attitudinal or emotional feeling about those who will benefit and those whose lives would be impossible if the breadwinner had died. We tend to avoid these harsh realities but it is the sensitivity and practicality of a great salesman that help us realise the significance and importance of buying life cover. Not many of us would buy from logic alone. Although it refers specifically to decisions about fitness and health, a research paper published in 2010[1] shows the impact of emotion upon decision making. It shows three elements to decision making, affect (emotion basically), cognition (the knowledge and logical side) and overall evaluation which includes the common sense aspects of value for money and "does it do what it says on the tin?" In essence the research demonstrates that affect and cognition impact upon overall decision making; however the interesting finding is that affect has a direct impact upon decision making whereas cognition 'feeds in' to overall decision making.

This alone may not be conclusive but it certainly supports our experience in selling and where we see improvements in sales through the affective or emotional and attitudinal responses of customers.

In the same journal another piece of research based upon people's intentions to save (financially) and care for the environment looked at the time aspect of the buyers' thinking.[2] This is relevant in many sales and was particularly true for Financial Services in that it looked at the idea of how committed a person was to a course of action dependent upon whether they took a long or short term view of the purchase (or other commitment). The "Attitude-Behaviour" piece in the title refers to the Attitude towards saving say and the Behaviour of actually doing what you intended. The findings showed that those with a longer term view were more likely to carry out the action or commitment. In selling this translates into a greater likelihood for people to buy if they have related their reason to buy to a longer term benefit. This may not be appropriate in all sales but we have seen many examples, including financial services where the longer term view has had a positive impact.

---

1   *The role of affect and cognition in health decision making*, Mario Keer, Bas van den Putte and Peter Neijens, British Journal of Social Psychology Volume 49, Part 1 pages 143-153

2   *Time perspective and Attitude-Behaviour consistency in future oriented Behaviours*, Anna Rabinovich, Thomas Morton and Tom Postmes, British Journal of Social Psychology Volume 49, Part 1 pages 69-89

Some responses can be quite "wow" or emotional and the sales person must not be fazed by this but equally he must be sympathetic and empathetic as far as he can. Often that longer term view can make a real difference: "how will it be, sitting on this terrace on a summer's day with a glass of your favourite tipple?" or "how will you feel when you have that lump sum when your son is ready to go to university or whatever he chooses to do?" Most people have enough imagination and "affective" awareness to be able to look at this future state and be influenced by it. The questions that help direct the customer's view to the future must relate to their reason for buying in the first place. Remember the impact of a 'custard' question!

Although we have experience that shapes our views on the depth of rapport that can be established in a sales conversation we are firm believers in building a relationship and gaining some form of "connection" with the customer. All that we have really explored in the era of ambition builds upon the earlier eras and consolidates, enhances and deepens the possibilities of building that connection with a customer. For some people it is part of their natural character to engage in this way, others may have to work at it but it is a learnable skill and provided the attitude is correct it will work. We are all aware that some "sincerity" is faked and sometimes undetectable as such. Where the sincerity is genuine it works better and more strongly and a greater connection is created. Not every customer will become a best friend and that is not what we are seeking or recommending, but it does ease the passage say from customer to consistent customer or client, defined as a customer who returns to buy from us again. The salesman's purpose is to sell and most buyers are aware of this but if the salesman is genuinely and sincerely interested in their client the sale is more likely to be secure and the connection is more likely to be deeper and more meaningful.

We make no apology for repeating the message that the open questions serve not only to help the salesman explore genuine 'needs and wants' but also to establish a connection and openness between salesman and customer. This is more likely to result in the customer feeling confident that what they are buying is really suitable and is, where appropriate, likely to result in repeat business. We have also seen that research supports the value of the approach using open questions in that they explore both the emotional and future thinking of the customer. So questioning, listening, interest and genuine conversation can produce the results the salesman seeks.

One thing we cannot answer is "How many open questions should we ask?" The honest but unsatisfactory answer is "enough". To gauge "enough" is an art developed from experience but a person listening and interested in people will usually get close to being right most of the time. We have found that some personality types respond to lots of questions, others are best only being asked one or two. A skilled questioner and listener can gain a lot from one question and that is why the openness of the relationship can often work so well. Being bothered to create some form of relationship can often be a differentiator. So it goes beyond the difference of whether you make a sale or not and can mark you as a salesman and your organisation as different, possibly superior to others.

Fortunately the quality salesmen and quality products and services shone through and customers came to respect both. The referral process was about asking satisfied customers if they knew of anyone else that may benefit from the types of products and services they themselves had just bought. Most would be able to think of at least one person and some could think of more. Some were more comfortable being the one to contact their friend to make the referral but others were happy to give the salesman the lead and contact details. Informally a system of referrals builds as one customer recommends another or more.

This too is the basis of a network, something we probably take for granted these days. Networking was beginning to emerge as a web of contacts who could help you directly or whom you could help directly in providing contacts and business leads. The important thing that also emerged with networking was the old fashioned concept of "as ye sow, so shall ye reap!" In other words time spent in developing a great network is valuable and also giving to the network leads to receiving. Networking and referrals certainly do produce great opportunities but we learned that it is not a one way street.

Coupled with this concept was the idea of making a customer a client. It is easy to see these as being the same but by our definition they are not. Here we mean a customer to be a "one-time" buyer whereas a client is one who comes back again, is keen to buy a new or different product and may contact you as the salesman. In other words some form of relationship has built. All this emerged before the concept of Customer Relationship Management and some of the complex software that that entails. On the formal side of the relationship it did probably start with a card index and gradually migrated to some form of software package. It may have included such things as adding a client to the infamous "Christmas card list" but the idea was something deeper than that. These were often a mainstay and would also be a good referral point as they typified a "good" customer. Having clients as opposed to a whole string of customers may be taken as a mark of success in that it indicated the salesman's integrity and was an endorsement of the products and services he was selling.

This could only happen if the salesman was selling to the true needs of the customer. As we have already said because of the nature of the product we are discussing here, the customer may not have expressed a need at the outset. The use of open questions would help in establishing the need in the customer's own mind too.

From here the concept would be to find the appropriate product in the portfolio that best matched that need. The converse of this matching of needs was that the salesman may over or undersell. In other words the possibility of selling too much or a product that is too "big" for the customer's needs or selling something that did not provide the adequate cover or protection for the customer and his family. The latter may emerge only at the time of the need actually arising and the customer or his family suffering as a result. The former may stretch the budget too far and disincline the customer from coming back for more when it is necessary.

Selling to needs was always a delicate balance; get it wrong and you could either let a customer down badly or turn them away, get it right and you would give them reassurance, comfort and relaxation in their mind. Also by getting it right you had a greater chance of turning a customer into a client. So all the Skills, Knowledge, Behaviour and Attitudes came to play here in making a success of the sale.

We have talked in earlier sections about understanding the motivation of the buyer. Here it was critical to understand the personal motivations and ambitions of the individual customer or client to ensure needs were matched and that they were satisfied and comfortable with what was sold to them. Even before high levels of regulation were brought into this market place, the successful salesman was almost self-regulating, realising that the concept of over or underselling or even misselling were counterproductive in the longer term.

Again it may be necessary to help the customer explore and elaborate upon his own needs and articulate them not only to the salesman but to himself too. Confirming with the customer that this was what he wanted to achieve allowed the matching of needs...needs that were driven by a personal motivation. In the case of life insurance sales one may say that the motivation was based upon a feeling or a need for security or "peace of mind".

One thing that emerged continuously but perhaps became prevalent in the era of ambition was self-confidence. For the true salesman in this era there were all the challenges of people buying what they wanted and when they wanted and having all the qualities and attitudes we described before, such as perseverance was never more important. Self confidence comes from so many things but is not least built upon by success, self belief, belief in product and service and through Skills and Knowledge, feeling comfortable and confident that the customer was likely to buy.

In turn this confidence led to the ability to assume a close. Obviously in an environment where the potential buyer was making decisions, it was all the more important to gain their commitment to buying "your product". Assumed closes can lead to "no" or objections if they are based upon a false understanding. So it was important to feel that the close was likely to lead to "yes" and the confidence to do this came from the open questions and building the need in the customer's own mind.

The assumed close in its simplest form was talking in the positive and as if the customer had already bought the service or product. In our example of life insurance we could see such phrases as these working as assumed closes:

- "So this is for Sally's university fees"

- "Mary is the beneficiary if anything happens to you and you the beneficiary if anything happens to Mary"

- "So this monthly investment ensures security for you all"

The idea here being that in your mind as the salesman, having done all the preparatory hard work you believe the customer will buy and so you talk as if they already have. It is essential however that you have done the background work and genuinely feel that the customer is ready to buy. Failure to do this will lead to objections or even a flat "no".

One of the toughest environments in which to use this method was the sale of life insurance where the customer was still a bit doubtful over the value or need.

There are again so many definitions of the close, where it happens and what it really is. Let us define here a trial or exploratory close. By this we mean finding out a reaction from the customer to a proposal before we make it or a derivation of it the final proposal. These trial closes, which can easily become the final close, are often best, in our experience, being alternative closes. Put simply the classic alternative may be exemplified by colour choice: "do you prefer the red or the blue?" It is easy to see this as part of the "funnelling" process of establishing true needs and wants. This technique also lends itself well to the objection handling and opportunity rebuilding. In our travel example it could be something like:

Salesman: I understand how you feel about travelling from Birmingham. The opportunities are a shorter transfer and a longer time in resort from the Manchester flight than the Birmingham flight that you had in mind. How do you feel about the transfer time and longer time in resort?

This is a trial or exploration which in essence is "which do you prefer, the convenience of Birmingham or the convenience in resort of a shorter transfer PLUS extra time in resort?" Alternative closes can work very well ultimately and also are extremely valuable in the exploratory stages.

An interesting facet of confidence in selling is the use of silence. Many people feel that silence is uncomfortable but if we can use silence judiciously as salesmen it can be a very useful asset. We are not advocating long periods of silence as that is likely to make a potential customer feel uncomfortable. However with some of the open questions we have suggested earlier it is advisable to allow the customer time to answer. By their very nature, open questions encourage reflection and time to ponder. If as the salesman we "jump in" to fill a silence or, worse still answer for the customer with our own observation or response we will destroy the value of the question. Of course customer personality type is relevant here as the driver may not want time but the analytical may need time to think, pause and reflect. It is not possible to say how long one should stay quiet as it is a matter of judgement and depends upon the conversation of which it is part. Usually we can tell if the customer is thinking about it and as long as we think they are thinking, we should give them time.

When we feel comfortable with silence or judging how and when to use it, we can encourage a customer to tell us more in response to an open question. Sometimes we may receive a response and it is appropriate to remain quiet to "tease" out a fuller response from the customer. Again this has to be a matter of judgement and is part of the art of being a salesman.

We realise that so much of what we do and talk about here is based upon being able to work with, deal with and understand people but we honestly believe that is part of the craft of a skilled salesperson. These crafts are learnable and really have to be tried and tested and blended into one's own way of doing things. An automaton salesperson who follows a set of rules rigidly will struggle. We have always offered guidelines and ideas and never a script or prescription as this is about an individual working with other individuals and is therefore dynamic. However, we have found those that use our guidelines or follow our suggestions tend to be more successful than those who do not.

Obviously you cannot match exact features and benefits to an individual in an introduction and you cannot assume that your product will be a panacea to them but carefully positioning the "global" benefits you aim at grabbing the potential customer's attention.

We have all experienced the attempts which come from a belief that 'our' product or service is the panacea: "I want to talk to you about how XYZ can really make a big impact for you." The interesting thing about the attention grabbing approach is that it is really a ten second, or less, 'elevator pitch' and starts from the probable issue or problem of the customer. In financial services most people would be interested in learning how to make or save money and secure their future, but not all. The key is to know the 'positioning' of your product or service and the issues or problems it is designed to overcome. It is also important to treat your customer as intelligent rather than someone who is definitely in need of your help. As customers we are more likely to respond favourably and listen to someone from the electricity company that says "I am calling from Electro Company. I just wanted to make sure you were aware of the opportunities to get the best tariffs for your utility bills". An approach that says "I am calling from Gas Corp and I want to help you save money" may be perceived as patronising and pushy.

As we said a moment ago, not all customers will want to listen and as a salesman we must not expect a high success rate; if we are not successful we may learn from that but we should not spend too long in what can become a reflexive downward spiral. Successful salesmen often invite the boss along to get feedback on what is working and what is not; that independent view can affirm good things and point to changes.

Probably the most significant learning as salesmen from the era of ambition was establishing the reason to buy. That is not just for the salesmen to be clear why their customer wants or needs to buy but, perhaps more significantly for the customers themselves to articulate and acknowledge their reasons for buying. If we consider that in this era people were in the frame of mind that said "I can have what I want and I'll live for now". The idea of future and understanding 'real' needs as opposed to wants and desires was anathema to many. The skilled salesman had to help the customer realise what they truly needed and to articulate that and feel happy that it was a true need! This was achieved through the use of open questions aimed at Attitudes and the more emotional aspects of the need. These questions encouraged a deeper relationship between the salesman and the customer through a simple process that generated a greater feeling of interest and felt more conversational. Clearly the salesman could make asking of questions a process driven aspect of selling but the art here is to make it conversational and show genuine interest in what the customer is saying.

The emphasis here is on asking the questions but the reality and the difference between an ordinary and a great salesman is the listening and interest in the customer's responses that accompany the questions. These together encourage the customer to be more open and to explore his own feelings and Attitudes and get to the deeper level of understanding why he really wants to buy.

It may be likened to the dreaded New Year Resolutions that so many people declare and fail upon just a few days into January. People would stick at them if they had explored the real reasons and therefore the benefits of the resolution, or alternatively realising it has no benefit and rejecting it earlier...just as useful for a salesman rather than battling to "no sale". The trouble with resolutions is that generally we do not have someone encouraging us to explore deeper the real reasons for undertaking it. A typical example might be "I want to lose weight; I am *going to* lose weight". If the resolver had a salesman selling the idea of losing weight the conversation may go like this:

Resolver: *I am going to lose weight*

Salesman: *What difference will losing weight make to you?*

Resolver: *I will feel fitter and I'll be able to get up stairs without puffing and panting*

Salesman: *What else will it mean to you?*

Resolver: *Well I'd be able to get into a smaller size of jeans and maybe I'd wear smaller tops too*

Salesman: *How would that make you feel?*

Resolver: *Brighter, healthier, more energetic, more enthusiastic, happier I guess.*

Salesman: *Sounds like it is important to you. When will you start?*

O.K. so we still need to examine how much weight, by when and how we would go about it but we have established some pretty important reasons to lose weight and this may well be the first time the "resolver" (customer) has thought about it in those terms and more likely the first time they said it out loud and with a witness. The incentive to buy, and stick with weight loss is greatly increased because it is no longer about losing weight but about feeling brighter, healthier, happier, more energetic and more enthusiastic.

The reason to buy is probably taking "motivation" to a deeper level. If we think of cost as not just being financial we can explore the reason to "buy" for so many things. Why are we spending time writing this book? Why are you spending time reading it? What difference will it make to your approach to selling?

The reason to buy, as we said before is probably one of the most significant aspects of encouraging a customer to buy from us rather than someone else. Again practise of the skill is needed and one will not be immediately proficient but it is worth pursuing.

You may have noticed a gentle start to a close in the "weight" scenario above too. "It sounds important to you. When shall we start?" Sometimes it may be better to separate the statement and question. Using the statement as almost a rhetorical question in this type of conversation has a good chance of gaining a positive response like "yes, it is important, it will be great to achieve". Then the assumptive but gentle "when shall we start?" or other appropriate expression that flows in the conversation can prompt the business to be concluded.

From that we can take a final step which cements the sale and completes the process. We usually refer to this as "waterproofing the sale" and it happens in so many different ways according to the sale. In financial services, for example it will include paperwork but more importantly reinforcing the value like "This is Tom's nest egg for when he starts university" or "This is the security for your wife and family". It is the practical piece but more importantly it is reinforcing the value to the customer based upon their reason for buying.

In our weight example from before, waterproofing may be along the lines of: "So this is the plan to get you underway towards feeling happier and healthier." The idea is to reinforce the value of the sale but very rarely it may also bring an objection, especially from the indecisive and cautious type. This gives us as salesmen another chance to help the customer see the opportunity as being bigger than the cost.

Our experience in sales and helping others improve their sales performance is that the techniques we have outlined build a greater connection with the customer, a need which only becomes more obvious as we will see in the next chapter. The salesman benefits because he is more likely to get the results he is after and the customer benefits because he ends up with something he really needs and wants *and* he walks away feeling he has been treated well. The changing Attitude of customers in the eras we have discussed already had to be matched and responded to and they were, by the *successful* salesman.

Confidence and individualism or independence and freedom were key characteristics that had gradually emerged over the years since the Second World War and customers reflected this ever more strongly as time was passing. Changes in company behaviour were beginning to map on to this too. Marketing people had taken great steps towards ensuring brand differentiation, personality and values were appealing and organisations expected their employees, especially those in direct contact with the customers, to live to and uphold these values. Sales people had realised that working to understand the true needs of customer and selling to those needs and wants was crucial to their success. They bothered to understand "where their customer was coming from" and attempted to "get on the same page" or "sing from the same hymn sheet" as customers so that some level of connection or *rapport* was built with them.

Successful salesmen realised that there were new Skills and Knowledge to acquire although none (or few) of the old had to go. Like many things in life, changes and growth occur but basic principles still apply. A jumbo jet takes off, alters direction and lands using the same principle as the Wright brothers used in Kitty Hawk all those years before. We can see that both are aeroplanes but the jumbo and the Wrights' plane are so different. So too with sales; the approach of a salesman in the times of the Wright brothers would be very different from the modern salesman. Likewise the changes in flight since the Second World War have been exponential and the changes or modernisation of good and successful sales practices have been on the same journey.

The significant thing for us all to be aware of is that "the world does not stand still" and these changes are continuous. Great for salesmen because there are always new things to sell, but equally there are new approaches to selling as the customer Attitude, Knowledge and awareness changes!

A summary

This era was one in which individuals owned more things and were in a situation where they could choose ownership more easily. The focus was more on the here and now than the long term. This is quite a lengthy chapter which in itself reflects the changes and the rapid, expansive progression in this era.

The Focus in this era

In this era we used our example of Financial Services and in particular the selling of life insurance to individuals and families. This was an era in which our progression was rapid and expansive as we had to apply many new approaches to selling at this time.

Motivation and Expectations

Individuals lived for the day and they had little thought, generally, for the longer term and the thought or need for life insurance was anathema to them so the salesman had to earn his crust.

Brand

The concept of brand was growing to be more like it is today. Marketing was emerging as a strategic aspect of many organisations. The then 5 P's of marketing took on significance and marketing added to the brand and generally became involved into selling by defining USP's (Unique Selling Proposition).

Key elements of selling

As was said before, this was an era where progression accelerated and expanded. In the areas of Behaviours and especially Knowledge and Skills new or developed concepts appeared. The original elements remained exactly as we described them in the earlier chapters. We will outline changes and additions here.

Behaviours

- Increased Awareness

In this era it became very important to be more aware of the needs and approaches of customers

- Availability to Customers

During this era it was beginning to be important to be available to a customer at times convenient to them. The 24 / 7 culture was just beginning

Attitudes

As Behaviours follow Attitudes, sales people needed to ensure open mindedness

Skills

- Personality and Behaviour identification

Our search went through the deep understanding that it helps a salesman to operate in an appropriate way dependent upon the customer behaviour and personality

- Open Questions

One of the greatest tools a salesman can have is the ability to use open questions to establish needs

- Opportunity is Bigger than the Cost

Creating in the mind of the customer the concept of the true value of the product or service being sold compared to the 'cost' measured in either money, time, effort, loss of face or change of mind.

Knowledge

Knowledge to support the Skills, Behaviours and Attitudes is always important especially, in this era, knowledge of behavioural types

Reflections

Putting all this together was important and in this section we reflect upon how all the changes in the Era of Ambition came together to help us progress rapidly in the sales arena.

The Parable of Bill Douglas D.F.C.
as told by Barrie Smith

It was 1979 and I had entered the financial services industry – "selling to business people in business hours" the advertisement said, but we were entering the era of ambition when sales were to be made any where at any time.

Whilst I had a number of years in sales, and a successful track record in selling in the grocery trade, I was used to making calls and sales on a pre-ordained list of businesses that needed my products – and selling financial services to a suspicious public was a whole new challenge.

The first few weeks were purgatory. Prospects were nowhere to be seen – but I was surrounded by them. Nobody wanted my products but everybody needed them. I was going in ever decreasing circles – and going nowhere very successfully.

What to do – no sales meant no income!

And under pinning this scenario was something I had never experienced previously – fear of failure! With that had come a loss of confidence and fear of even talking to people. Getting up in the morning to find people to talk to who didn't want me near them was the scariest scenario I could envisage.

At this point Bill Douglas was appointed as my Sales Manager and was about to change my career and life.

Bill had been a pilot in RAF Bomber Command during the Second World War. He had twice been shot down by enemy gunfire, ditched into the sea and got himself and his crew back to England safely for which he had been awarded the DFC on two occasions. Not that Bill ever talked about those years – except occasionally over a glass or two of whisky when in the company of other service men particularly if they had been in Fighter Command!

My first meeting with Bill was so low key I was astounded. I had been expecting a searching examination of my efforts and subsequent failures.

Instead I was asked some question,

"Have you managed to book one appointment since you have been with us'?"– the answer was of course yes.

"How did you do it?" Bill asked. I explained how it had been achieved.

"Were you scared before you did it?" How did he know? Yes I replied

. "Could you do it again?" Bill asked. The answer had to be yes - my newly appointed mentor had faced much greater challenges than talking to a few prospects.

I left that meeting inspired – and determined. Yes I still had some fear but everything is relative.

Just before I left Bill had explained that to be successful all I had to do was book four appointments with prospects every day. One of these appointments would be cancelled and if I saw three people every day success was certain to follow.

The next day I had a call from Bill – "Evening Barrie – did you get your four? Thanks to his inspiration I was able to say yes.

That call came every day for the next few weeks – of course the answer wasn't always yes but during those conversations I was never once asked if I had made a sale. The conversation was always about activity and booking appointments. Of course it was me who talked about the sales I had made – all Bill said to that was "good"

Bill had taught me some vitally important lessons,

- Never be afraid of failure – everything is relative and there are greater fears to overcome

- You cannot manage results – you can only successfully manage activity.

- Know your ratios – they will be a predictor of success

In the months that followed Bill increased my Knowledge of ratios and the importance of keeping accurate records of those numbers – from the simple 4 Appointments will bring 3 meetings (On average) to a complete record of:

Approaches Made – Appointments Booked – Appointments Kept – Presentations Made –

Closes Attempted – Sales Made – Commission Earned.

This enabled me know how much I would earn by simply attempting to book an appointment and so predicting the income for the weeks and months ahead.

I have shared this story with many aspiring sales professional over the years and, as a result, there are many successful individuals besides myself who owe Bill Douglas DFC and Bar a quiet glass of Malt.

THE ERA OF REALISM

In which we see how customers have the capability to be better informed and in which we see how customers have developed their own Buying Process and we introduce selling techniques to meet this challenge

Background to the era

A change of century, new ideas, new hopes, new ambitions, new dreams but still more of the same. We are not whizzing around with jet-packs on our backs but virtual worlds and technology may make it feel as though we have that capability. Information and knowledge are ubiquitous and our laptops take the pain of spelling and grammar away from us; even looking up the meaning of words can be done on-line.

Some things have gone almost back in the circle, but the circle is different. In England post-war we had a succession of Prime Ministers who had been public school educated; we then went a long time with Prime Ministers who were grammar school educated but now our "leaders" are from public schools again. Yet the world they inhabit and the challenges they face are very different from those facing Prime Minister Eden, Macmillan and so on in the era of consolidation.

Life changes so quickly that we struggled to settle on a title for this section. Clearly this is the age of information with folks holding their lives in a mobile device that provides e-mail, diary, phone, internet connection in a small hand held "device" and with books now selling in electronic format to be read on some form of electronic tablet. It is also rapidly transforming into an age of realism as people understand that money is not so freely available, buying has to be more carefully considered and governments are making tough choices which the populace either understands and supports or rebels against.

Despite this reality, life continues and people continue to buy, albeit with greater care and caution. This creates all the more reason for the sensitive and ethical salesman to help people in this process.

As the population increases in size in the UK, it is also ageing with the "baby boomers" of the post Second World War era reaching retirement age. Health and opportunities to sustain health are increasing and people generally take their health, fitness and well-being more seriously than before. Legislation has been designed to help this through such initiatives as preventing smoking in public houses, restaurants and so on. Initiatives to reduce alcoholic consumption have so far been less successful and interestingly cigarette consumption is still relatively high, though a more private occupation. With this backdrop forecasts suggest that the population of Britain in 2021 will have five per cent aged eighty years or older.

Advances in medical science allow people to live longer but as yet cures for the degenerative illnesses and mental depreciation have not kept to quite the same pace. An ageing population, perhaps more dependent upon those in work to provide the nation's wealth increases the need for the country to have a vibrant economy. Changes are being made to the statutory retirement age and more people are living alone than before with a higher rate of divorce.

The world suffers from a recession that nobody seemed able to predict or forestall and the political and economic debates as to the best solution prevail. Our only comment will be that we still need sales and professional sales people in such an environment and we contend that selling will help us through the situation. With greater caution at both a corporate, organisational and individual level, the pressures on the skills and abilities of both marketers and salesmen are increasing.

The good news is that people still have a sense of humour and humanity continues. Early in the new century popular television included such things as "Only Fools and Horses" or "The Vicar of Dibley" or comedy dramas such as "Auf Wiedersehen Pet". Although quite different from the comedy workshops and comic talent shows of years before, the 2000's saw a real re-emergence of the stand up comic with "Live at the Apollo" or "An Evening with…." as examples.

Sport continued to be popular too with Rugby World Cups drawing good audiences as did Football as witnessed by the growth of the Premier League.

There was also a rise in the quest for instant success through such programmes as Pop Idol or The X-Factor. Celebrity and minor celebrity was evident in programmes like "I 'm a Celebrity, Get me Out of Here" or "Strictly Come Dancing" and the competitive nature of humans demonstrated through such programmes as "Master Chef" or the combination of two concepts in "Celebrity Master Chef". Envy or awe ensued as the less talented saw sportsmen who won medals or cups in their sport go on to excel in dancing or cooking or both.

Paparazzi, although not new phenomena, were and are significant and probably enjoyed the opportunity arising from the public interest in celebrity. The name actually originates from an Italian dialect and refers to the "annoying noise produced by a mosquito". The term Paparazzi had entered the English psyche way back in the 1960's and has come to mean the intrusive photojournalist. In the newer understanding of the word Paparazzi had opportunities in print as well as on the electronic media and reflected the ubiquity of information welcomed, needed or helpful or not, upon which the world in the twenty first century seemed to depend.

The nature of "pop" music has changed too with the use of Internet and the small and smaller devices upon which music could be recorded and played back. These MP3 players enabled the user to download an entire album, individual tracks or to formulate their own collections or "playlists". Far from the vinyl records of the 1960's freedom of choice also encouraged illegal down loading and changes in legislation as well as practicalities had to be made. The nature of a "hit" also changed as it gradually came to include download sales as well as physical CD purchase and the volume of sales that result in a "gold" or "platinum disk" have changed.

Music was more global perhaps with some old favourites"remaining popular but probably regenerating themselves, for example Madonna or Kylie Mynogue but the emergence of bands such as Cold Play, The Black Eyed Peas, Mumford and Sons, typifying a spectrum perhaps and individuals such as Lady Gaga, Pink, Will Young (a winner in Pop Idol) and Nellie Furtado for example. Different genres of music also had their 'day in the sun' as they were more available to a wider audience. Country, folk, dance, rap, electronic and jazz or blues all had recognition as well as the more generic rock or popular music of the era. Also the historical stock of music was continuously added to and stored so Sinatra, Crosby (Frank and Bing) and The Beatles were still aired.

Technology was in profusion with more homes having a personal computer and access to the invasive Internet. Rivals in providing broadband services, mobile phones and more channels for television including High Definition and the ability to pause "live" broadcasts emerged and competed.

Focus in this era

In the era of knowledge and realism we turn our attention to selling consultancy. Consultancy is generally used by organisations when they are short of time, expertise or enthusiasm for a particular project. What is significant in this highly competitive market is that the consultant needs to be aware of reputation, the importance of understanding true needs and clarity of purpose.

As you have probably already imagined most of the consultancy work we have been involved in has been to improve sales performance and we can honestly report that we have had great success. We have also been involved in customer service and customer retention work and all have a common theme.

One thing that is noticeable is that most of the selling practices we have discussed and explored are suitable in all environments and apply to all products and services. The difference is Product Knowledge but the approach is quite common. Our experience has re-emphasised the importance of referrals and networking, but nonetheless one has to demonstrate "why me rather than someone else". With a plethora of consultants all peddling expertise it is essential that we are different *and* that we provide true value and success. The practicalities of the market place and the range of our customers keep us aware and ensure we are right up to date with all we offer.

These are lessons that we share openly with clients and help us to keep abreast of and understand the significance of customer requirements.

It is through this process that we have come to understand where the customer truly is in this "process" of selling and because of this we formulated the customer perspective in a buying process whereby the great and successful salesmen will arrive at "Congruence". We will elaborate these further but suffice to say that we have seen great success where these approaches have been warmly embraced.

Bringing these strands of thoughts together we can see that customers are potentially more knowledgeable or aware; they are also more cautious about making a value for money, 'right' decision in what they buy and these two criteria alone make demands upon the salesmen.

Previously we talked about needs and the ability to help customers and clients explore their own true needs or "reason to buy". This is really evident in the era of realism where the pressure not to buy is perhaps stronger than it has been for a very long time. Individuals and organisational buyers may have very different needs and different pressures upon them and their expectations may be very different too. An aware and sensitive salesman will be assimilating all of this through conversation and questioning so that he really understands the customer and how he can help him with his product and service.

We can fully understand why some salesmen feel daunted by the current market conditions and why some almost capitulate and throw their hands up in horror. Probably the ratios (calls to sales at its simplest level) are changing in many cases and revenues and volumes are not what they were. However the market still exists and if we really can take a customer centric approach and help them to make buying decisions we can continue to succeed.

In essence we have seen a shift over time where the salesman instead of "pushing" product is now enabling the customer to buy. Our approach to the "buying" process is the common theme in all environments in fact and we have found that there are subtle differences to sales processes to allow them to match the buying process. No matter to whom we are selling, the approach is individual and unique. This requires that salesmen avoid formulaic approaches. In fact we never recommend a scripted approach, preferring a structure which gives flexibility and opportunities for the salesman to treat everyone individually.

Expectations and Motivations

In a time of realisation that we needed to be more careful about what we spent and with governments looking carefully at their expenditure the overall motivation had to be one of seeking "value for money". In the last section we discussed the importance of selling to needs and wants; in the era of realism that is all the more important. Even before the more "straightened" times, there was another key factor that drove many people. That was that they needed to acquaint themselves with products and services, often in quite detail and examining the competitive offerings long before they would "come" to buy. With information readily available on the internet many customers would research services and products and be quite knowledgeable before the salesman could begin to talk with them. The danger for the customer and the salesman alike was the classic 'a little learning is a dangerous thing'. Often it would be difficult to make direct comparisons as the information could be on different bases and may only headline certain features or prices. This could mean that a customer believes a competitor is offering the same "thing" at a lower price while the truth is that the service and product is quite different.

This has an impact upon the salesman's motivation in the sales environment in that they have to ensure that the customer is fully aware of the features and benefits of their product. It also means that awareness of competitor offerings has to be sharper and absolutely accurate. Furthermore the skill in addressing issues where the customer has the wrong end of the stick has to be handled sensitively. So the background to the sale has an added complexity; add to that some of the realisations that have occurred to us over the recent years and we can see that selling is the same yet quite different from before.

We have added to our store and awareness of the Behaviours, Attitudes, Skills and Knowledge that differentiate the successful salesman from the rest. We have not thrown out the baby with the bathwater and have retained many of the traditional "techniques" in our approach. Like all change, somebody starting out now will accept the new landscape and change as time goes on and new demands are made.

In essence the motivation today is different from when this journey started but has similar elements: the salesman wants to sell and the buyer wants to buy, but they are more knowledgeable and want to buy only if things represent value for money and truly meet their needs.

Brand

Subtle yet strong, each brand has to differentiate itself from others not only in terms of product offering and service but in style too. By style here we mean such things as personality, image, characteristics and values. One of the things that customer knowledge has brought is the potential for commoditisation or the notion that "they're all the same". Brand owners, managers and creators now have to demonstrate more subtle ways in which *their* product or service is different. This has been there in the past but is now more necessary given the need to show value and differentiation to convince a customer that this brand is more suitable for them than another.

Some brand loyalties are generated locally, some globally and some combine both. We don't intend to elaborate upon different brands and their values, but consider how Manchester United Football Club has a local following as well as a global image that attracts people far and wide to buy the latest season's shirts and other merchandise. Consider too how the various supermarket chains in the UK advertise in one way on price comparison but in other ways extolling differences in product and quality of service. Notice too how service has changed such that most stores now deliver grocery orders placed on-line, as are books, CD, DVD, electronic goods - the list is long and growing.

Brand carries a concept of reputation too. Reputation comes in many forms and can be a prized 'possession'. We talked before of referrals for new business; this is the classic value of a reputation. It happens in so many ways and at so many levels. For example you may have just had your house repainted externally and visitors, friends are thinking of having theirs done. You may be an ambassador for 'your' decorator in terms of quality, timeliness, cleanliness, unobtrusiveness and so on. 'Your' decorator has projected a brand image and created a positive reputation in your eyes so you are happy to recommend him.

Similarly you may have had a refitted kitchen and friends notice it. It has been carried out through a nationally known company and the quality of product, the service and so on was such that you can recommend them. Equally it is not impossible to conceive of situations where we do not recommend or even give negative word of mouth reports. Brand image, reputation and values carry with each individual contact and the opportunity and cost formula reappears at each turn, not always being about price.

Some branding is price based and we can be clear when it is, but oftentimes the modern customer will look through "false" economies although sometimes it may well be that some people are compelled to buy the cheapest product. The challenge is to demonstrate the value (opportunity) of our own product and sometimes that may mean that purchase has to be deferred and the buyer or customer needs to save in order to buy a more expensive product.

It is worth considering the brands that each of us may represent, in whatever capacity. What are the brand values? What is the image or 'personality' our brand is trying to portray? What is our reputation in the market? What has created that reputation? As a salesman, how do I and can I maintain or enhance the brand I represent? Do I conform to the brand values and image myself?

We are all aware too that brand has become highly individualised as we see "celebrities" creating brand around themselves or being employed as the "face" of a brand. For example we think of "Brand Beckham" or Woods, Henry and Federer representing Gillette. Also the Virgin brand is almost synonymous with Richard Branson and yet covers a whole range of products and services.

The key elements of selling

In this section we will explore the new or changed elements of Behaviour, Attitude, skill or Knowledge required by the successful salesman in the era of reality. It is also worth a reminder that previous elements that were important remain important in this era too although we may modify them slightly here with new learning and understanding of the "climate" in which sales are being made. We will build up the more significant changes and developments here.

Behaviours

- *Networking*

We have already discussed the significance of networking and referrals to gain new business. The significance here is that as part of a differentiator and showing the value that one can add, the network needs to be assured of success, value for money and results more than ever before. The network is still one of the most valuable assets but is increasingly "critical" or "evaluative" as everyone has to justify expense and demonstrate value and results.

 It therefore becomes imperative in the market where customers and clients are more "picky" and Knowledgeable that we treat them and understand them as individuals. The network is not a single entity but a group of individuals or different organisations requiring different approaches and unique understanding.

There is also the significance of increasing the network of which one is a part. The increasing use of social networking and business networking on line should and can be used, judiciously! Comments, blogs or blog responses remain forever and can easily be found on search engines so whilst the extension of a network can be useful, it needs to be done with awareness of what one is saying and the impression one is creating.

• *Adapting to modern communication methods and styles*

Some use of mobile technology may have gone over the top. Imagine the scene of a couple in a restaurant on St Valentine's Day and each is on a mobile phone! Are they talking to each other? It is a scene most of us have witnessed but with whom were they talking? However, realistically staying in touch has become increasingly important and the pace of life demands that we are connected for a good proportion of our day.

The salesperson who is working remotely from his office needs to be in touch for updates, to give feedback and to receive "new opportunities". It is also important to be accessible to one's network as an opportunity may arise and it can be as critical as being available to respond that makes a difference.

With the increased availability of wireless connection, email available to phones or other hand held devices it has really become part of the remote and mobile communication we just referred to.

Email also allows for documentation to flow between recipients more rapidly so quotes, recommendations, brochures and so on can be exchanged quite speedily as befits the modern, pacy world. It allows what the Information Technology world refers to as asynchronous connection such that an individual may not have to be on-line but will pick up the e-mail and any attachments at a time convenient to him. It can be more direct, secure and generally faster than surface mail of the paper variety. Synchronous email (i.e. both parties on line simultaneously) allows for documents to be transferred, discussed and amended and approved "live".

Email can also be a barrier to the salesman as our potential buyer or prospect can ignore it and hide behind cyberspace.

There are an increasing number of shared space links that allow documents to be shared and modified on line live and "in front of your very eyes". The upshot of this is that people no longer have to be in the same place to enact these transactions. This may work well in the modern world but it increases the need for accuracy in the written word as sadly we have all experienced emails that are misunderstood, misinterpreted or in which the "tone" is misread.

Social media are widely used too and some are totally business oriented whilst others are more social. However, people use these to promote themselves and ideas!

There is nothing that can truly replace a one to one meeting and exchange of views, concerns and ideas. That said email and social media are absolutely invaluable in the business world.

• Use of "the Web"

Web use may depend upon the nature of the business and can range from the simple electronic brochure to a full blown sales machine. People who access a website will do so for different reasons too but often it may be to check out the organisation, its reputation, reliability, integrity and possibly its clientele where appropriate.

It has become a requirement of modern business to have a website and it is not merely a marketing device as many sites offer opportunities to buy and all offer the opportunity to contact the organisation. The site can often show a lot more about the organisation in terms of experience and what it offers in general. It may not necessarily be the "sales tool" but it will, quite possibly, influence decisions. Quite. It is possible to make the whole process more of a "self help" situation and this may lose the personal contacts.

Attitudes

- *Consumer awareness*

There is probably not much more to say here other than that the individual salesman needs to be aware that he is no longer in the position of "strength" created from knowledge of one's own product and those of competitors. The attitude need not necessarily be that the customer is King, but a great respect for their awareness will result in a different approach towards the sale.

- *Customer as Knowledgeable purchaser*

Being aware that customers have access to a wide range of information is crucial. Being sensitive to the fact that they may have some misconceptions is critical and dealing with those without being superior or patronising is essential. Equally it is important to be aware that the customer may often be right and may have information that we as the sales people don't have. An open Attitude, accepting that customers are knowledgeable is important. That a customer can check on the salesman and the company proposition means that the salesman has to be accurate and factual with his information. This leads to the significance of our next point on customer knowledge.

- *Greater comparison between products and services*

Not only are customers more aware and better informed, information is more accessible and freely available to those who are shopping. As I have said, with the era of realism people are more likely to shop around to find value for money and as a result many are more cautious in their purchasing. As salesmen we need to be sensitive to that and be prepared to help shoppers to understand their own requirements properly and then be able to match our products or services to those requirements.

This aspect really has meant new skills for many people we have worked with and reflects a new understanding in the approach we have adopted too.

These Attitudes are really about being open to the changes that are happening in society. A closed mind and preserving a superior attitude will not be successful in the climate of the era of reality.

Skills

- *Heightened and advanced interpersonal communication*

We have always valued the importance of good interpersonal communication in selling and we have spent time here discussing the significance of asking good open questions to help the customer articulate their true needs. We have also advocated the importance and value of accurate listening (remember the custard questions?).

In the era of reality more than ever have those requirements become more acute and valued. The wary customer 'knows' a lot more and we need to listen very attentively to their needs and what they already 'know' so that we can match, and re-educate as necessary.

The re-education piece requires sensitivity as we do not want the customer to feel that we are correcting them! That demands careful choice of words, tone and delivery and is quite an advanced skill of interpersonal communication. We must never overlook the emotional content of what the customer says as that is often what determines the purchase decision.

We have probably all suffered the fate of being offered whatever the salesman has "on their books". We won't single out a profession here but we must all be mindful of careful listening and then responding to the customer's needs, clarifying them as we go. There is an easy temptation to think we have a potential buyer and so thrust everything we have under their nose. This is pretty much a guaranteed turn-off to the customer who may well think 'They never listened to what I really wanted' and become irritable. However it is possible to offer things as part of the clarification of understanding process. For example: "To help me understand exactly what you need, what do you feel about this one?" Otherwise it is to be avoided!

◆ Handling Objections

The above example may lead to the customer being turned off and "objecting".

Being bothered may be a sentiment we echo again and again. It matters too in the language we use; asking open and relevant questions, being on the customer's wavelength and explaining things without jargon. It also matters in handling objections; one may say it *especially matters* in handling objections as this is a second chance and an opportunity to clarify or put right any earlier misunderstandings.

There are so many ways to handle objections but we have found this simple approach that generally works well with today's customers. The basic concept is to make the customer feel that they are not alone in having that objection and that others have resolved it in their minds. Whilst we may like to feel unique and special, most of us also have a very strong sense and desire to belong and feel part of a group. This methodology uses that tendency in order to be successful.

The method is referred to as "feel, felt, found" after the three key words that the salesman uses to begin to explore the objection and overcome it. We will examine this in detail in the "Reflections" section below.

- *Treating the customer as a Knowledgeable "partner" in the process*

As we have said, customers have increasing awareness and knowledge of what is available to them and so one of the proven concepts is to treat them as partners. The position of salesman all knowledgeable and powerful has gone and so the new idea is to treat customers as equal partners in the journey to helping them buy. A partnership implies equal respect and equal opportunity for a good outcome.

This probably was the greatest insight we had to sales in this era; that a mutual success is achievable in the process. The salesman gains a sale and the customer buys what they truly want and need, which surely must count as success on both sides.

It is a Skill as well as an Attitude and is fundamental, especially for those selling high value or highly valued services or products.

This forms the basis of the customer buying process which we will discuss shortly in the section on reflections. The skill is to ensure that we do help the customer through the process and do not short circuit it as that can lead to problems.

- *Use of multi media*

In the era of reality, as we already mentioned, the use of mobile and remote technology is paramount and the use of various types of software can be extremely advantageous. Contact records can be maintained on a database and presentations made using presentation software. Salesmen may also keep proposals and formal documents like requests for information or requests for pricing in word processing type software. Clearly the ability to use these with the increased independence and remote working in many organisations is useful. The use of laptops and other, smaller hand-held devices is increasing the need for people to be conversant with different solutions. There is also the need to be aware of how to use projecting equipment occasionally and even still the use of a presentation package that the client may receive, especially if you wish to leave something after a meeting.

* *Appropriate communication using the new media*

Not only is there the skill required for using the software and other tools, but also, more importantly the skill required to use it effectively to communicate. It is possible to have a great technical presentation for example which is really engaging but ruined by poor personal communication ability. There are different Skills too in standing up and making a formal presentation to a room full and making a more intimate one to one or one to small group presentation, sitting together at a table. The ability to be 'appropriate' can make critical differences in getting the information across to an audience.

Knowledge

* *Bringing all appropriate Knowledge together*

Bringing all the Knowledge together is very important. We have tried to include only the items in each era that are still relevant today in the era of reality. As you will see from the list below, there is not a huge variety in the Knowledge attached to successful selling. It is more to do with skilful application and good Attitudes and Behaviours. We have listed the Knowledge areas from earlier eras here as a reminder.

- *Product Knowledge*

- *Competitors Products*

- *Market Knowledge*

- *Political awareness*

- *Identifying "political levers"*

- *Personality style cues*

- *Open Question types*

Putting these together with the two "new" areas below will provide a salesman with the areas of Knowledge he will need in the era of realism. As ever, the latest additions make the difference to success or otherwise in the era in question, particularly the concept of the customer's buying process.

- *The sales to service continuum*

We have often worked with people who emphatically state "I am not a salesman" as if it were something quite alien to their role and possibly a personal taboo. They refer to themselves as service providers and perhaps their job title does include something about "customer service" or "customer support". What we have found though is that the line between sales and service is becoming more and more blurred. Customers expect before, during and after sales service and in their mind there is no difference between functions; they bought something and they want it supported regardless of who sold it and who supports it. In and of itself selling well and acknowledging the customer as a partner encourages classic customer service.

◆ The Buying Process

Throughout history people have always bought goods and services and this simple act has developed elements that have existed for a long time, and ultimately will not go away! So why does the buying process in this era of realism suddenly become so important? It is because, as never before, a buyer is better informed, more aware and more discerning whilst the propositions have become more varied, more complex and, in many cases have the potential to be life-changing.

It is against this background that the sales professional must ensure they work *with* their potential customer.

Reflections

We know that the landscape has changed. Customers are more knowledgeable and discerning about how they buy, perhaps even the smallest item, to ensure they are receiving value for money and good quality. With access to the internet and the increasing prevalence of "comparison" websites, customers are increasingly knowledgeable although many are still confused by the range of what's on offer. Many customers may narrow down one or two suppliers to approach and will have some knowledge and from that maybe more questions of a more detailed nature than we as salesmen might generally expect.

Most customers are well informed, discerning or careful in what they are buying and seek to get value for money. Again most customers do not want to be patronised and actually enjoy being treated as partners.

Our approach is designed entirely to engage the customer, treat them with respect and as a partner in the process. The open questions that the salesman asks are not leading or pressurising but designed to help the customer articulate his needs and wants in a coherent fashion. They are designed as well to help the customer reflect upon his own real reason for buying; it helps him to engage with the emotional side of the reason for his purchase decision.

In helping customers through their buying process and in helping them articulate their needs this approach addresses a lot of customer needs and is customer centric. What can lead it away from being customer centric is an absence of listening and the dreaded custard question or pushing our product or service regardless of what the customer needs.

Selling is a profession; sadly there may not be university courses in selling like other organisational functions but it is the lifeblood of commercial organisations. This may easily tempt a salesman to push and drive for the sale almost at any cost. We can understand that but everything we have built towards in our search has made us realise that the modern approach has to be more customer centric.

So how is this in the better interest of the salesman? If we consider that customers are well connected these days with social networks on the internet as well as the traditional face to face connections they are in a powerful situation to be our advocates or to speak against us. Their expectations and needs are more demanding than ever and their voice louder than ever, so it is in our interest to take notice of them and help to guide them to what *they* want.

The advantage is not just into the longer term although that has great value. The longer term advantages are: reputation, recommendation and referral, repeat sales, value and possible higher level sales in the future. The shorter term advantages are a more secure sale, less likelihood of objections, less likelihood of a change of mind during any "cooling off" period and potentially a higher value sale.

We have seen the Skills and to an extent the Behaviours, Attitudes and Knowledge grow and shift over the years. What remains consistent is that the salesman is valuable to his organisation; what ultimately and fundamentally is important is that the truly professional salesman is valued by his customer. This has always been the case but perhaps never more so than in the era of realism. Helping customers to decide what is truly right for them, meeting their needs, wants and desires is perhaps a different perspective on selling than when we started the journey but to us this is the excitement and joy that selling can provide.

Our experience has shown increased sales across a range of products and services by using this approach. It has increased the confidence of the salespeople we have encountered; it has helped to reduce customer "churn" and ultimately added to bottom line profitability.

In business there is probably no such thing as altruism, but if practicality shows that listening to customers, addressing their needs, concerns and apparent knowledge in an open way can lead to increased profitability then we believe it makes sense for all. We are seeing a greater success in sales where there is a greater sharing or equality between buyer and salesman.

In the spirit of equality we see a benefit from treating customers as individuals but not as solo travellers who are islands and disunited from others. In handling objections, building a need and creating "Congruence", language has to be carefully thought through. For example, where a customer is objecting to a purchase, for whatever reason, we need to handle the situation sensitively. Using insurance sales as an example:

Salesman: I understand how you *feel*. Several other customers have *felt* the same when looking at the level of cover. What they *found* was that when they looked at their income, expenditure and what would happen if the income stopped they really did need that level of cover.

The method firstly acknowledges and empathises with the customer's feelings. We have found that it is more to do with feelings at the possibility of getting it wrong or being sold something not wanted or "over the top". From the earlier quoted research it is apparent that feelings have greatest direct impact. Having acknowledged feelings we continue to "support" the customer in not feeling alone by showing that others have shared the same feelings of doubt. Finally we ask the customer to reconsider, as others in his circumstances did before, and look at the value of what we are offering.

We have found that *"feel, felt, found"* works for any product and service being sold and at least keeps the door ajar for further exploration. The *felt* and *found* aspects must relate to the objection raised.

We can sense a lot of people reading this saying at this point, "What a lot of pedantic fuss over such a small point". Well that is an objection that comes from a variety of places such as: been there, done it differently and it worked; I use "think" language and it's OK; it sounds silly; I can't say that; that's not my style and several others. All we can say is "We know how you feel. Many others we have introduced to this method felt the same. Interestingly they found when they tried it, it worked and kept the conversation open, giving them a second chance".

One temptation we can all easily fall for is to confront the customer and bamboozle them with competitor comparisons and heap on the features and benefits (perhaps as was the case in the era of consolidation). Yes of course that will work some of the time and we will feel good. It is, however, more advisable to avoid conflict with a customer and rather help them rebuild the need, value and opportunity in their own minds. It is possible that we may need to scale down our offering, but if we did our open questioning (or soft fact finding as we often refer to it) correctly that is unlikely or will be limited.

Whilst we are "on about" language you may have noticed that we are careful over the use of 'however' and 'but' in our objection handling, as we should be in any response to our customer. If we empathise we are on the same wavelength as the customer, however when we use the word 'however' or 'but' we are changing tack completely. The use of 'however' or 'but' in these circumstances can be like a slap in the face for the customer or can be tantamount to saying "I understand, but you are wrong" and then we're back into the confrontation scenario. Consider how we may come across if we were to change the wording of this travel example.

Salesman: I understand how you *feel*. I know that other travellers have *felt* the same about going from a different airport. What they *found* was that arriving at an airport closer to the resort so saving time on the transfer at the other end, and having almost a full day more in resort was worthwhile.

We now change the *found* sentence thus:

Salesman: I understand how you *feel*. I know that other travellers have *felt* the same about going from a different airport. **But** they *found* it was **worthwhile** saving in time on the transfer at the other end, and having almost a full day more in resort.

It is more confrontational and the empathy we built in the first two sentences is dissipated. Again some may say this is being pedantic and again we would respond by saying "We know how you feel. A great number of others felt the same when they first started to be careful with their language. What they found when they *were* more careful excited them because their results started to improve."

Remember that a *found* sentence addresses the benefit others have seen and that is a stated concern of the customer, going counter to their desires or needs. We have had to assume that you do want to improve your results....we trust that is a reasonable assumption.

The approach is supportive and, if delivered correctly, non-threatening and allows the buyer a face saving "escape" if absolutely necessary, still resulting in a sale but perhaps at a lower level. The salesman's sensitivity is critical here, especially as it may well be the absence of sensitivity or awareness that has led to the objection in the first place.

In this era we realised the importance of truly engaging the customers' concerns and using phrases that would engage without patronising them. The use of the words *feel, felt* and *found* is deliberate. We are focused on feelings here even if the objection is phrased from a more "thinking" based language. Most objections probably come from some form of emotional response and if we look back at the research we mentioned earlier, the emotional has a direct impact upon intention to act.

If we consider that the objection is raised because we have not helped the customer see the opportunity as being bigger than the cost then we do need to go back and help rebuild the real need, the reason to buy and that too, generally, comes with and from some emotional base. So that's where we start from by saying "I understand how you feel". Now it is probable that we are dealing with someone who is a "thinker" rather than a "feeler" so we do not dwell too heavily on the feeling piece. Yes we do repeat it in saying "other people felt the same" but soon we move to what they "found" which is thinking or feeling neutral.

The majority of objections, if not all, arise when the customer has not seen the "value" of what it is they are buying. We tend to refer to that value as being the "opportunity", meaning the opportunity the purchase will allow including changes in life style, comfort, security, peace of mind, convenience or luxury for example. The objection has resulted because the customer sees the cost as being greater than the opportunity. We need to point out that cost here does not only mean financial; it may also refer to convenience, time, replacing one activity with another and so on. In a travel example the customer may see that flying from Manchester is a cost in time, effort and convenience compared to flying from Birmingham. The opportunity may be that they have longer time in resort as the Manchester flight may take them to an airport where the transfer to resort is considerably less or it may even be that Birmingham flights do not coincide with the customer's travel dates.

The imperfections of our finding exact details, hard information, like dates and times, or attitudinal information, soft facts and emotional responses to the travel and the holiday coupled with the customer's preconceptions ("I must fly from Birmingham") can result in this objection. Objections are avoidable if you have listened very carefully, built a true understanding of the customer's needs and wants and offered alternatives to establish a response. However in the "real" world objections happen. What we have to do is rebuild the opportunity in the customer's mind so that it is seen as at least in proportion to the cost, or better still that it is seen as value for the cost.

Using our travel example here we may tackle it like this:

> Customer: *But I really want to travel from Birmingham. Manchester is really rather inconvenient.*

> Salesman: *I understand how you feel. I know that other travellers have felt the same about going from a different airport. What they found was that arriving in an airport nearer the resort and saving in time on the transfer at the other end, giving almost a full day more in resort was worthwhile.*

> Customer: *Yes I can see the sense in that, but I had hoped that Birmingham would be possible.*

> Salesman: *Yes, I know how you feel about that. What do you feel about having that extra time in the resort?*

And so it may continue exploring some of the aspects which in an ideal world would have been discovered in the open questioning earlier. However we are realists and we know that objections will be raised, we won't always explore everything in the initial "search" phase of a conversation and not all objections will be resolved. We do believe that these 'tools' and concepts will work considerably more often than not for a salesman.

The idea is that we try to establish the opportunity as being greater than the cost initially through establishing the hard factual information and the soft factual emotional responses and Attitudes.

If that has not worked we combine the feel, felt, found tool with re-establishing the value and opportunity in the customer's mind. The customer will balance the alternatives in his mind.

When it comes to it, the ultimate decision, "to buy or not to buy, that is the question" is the preserve of the customer. As a salesman we cannot "force" them to purchase from him or purchase at all. People are being more careful about decisions and feel more independent as they believe they are more Knowledgeable. The buying point is when that customer makes that decision and comes, probably when "Congruence" has been achieved. Not always will the decision go in favour of a purchase but our responsibility as salesmen is to enable that customer to make that decision based upon true knowledge, true awareness of their needs, wants and desires, and a real understanding of how well our product or service meets those needs, wants and desires.

To facilitate that responsibility a successful salesman will enable a customer to pursue their individual journey on the buying process. As we have said, the process may not be sequential every time, but in order to bring the customer to a point of willingness or action and "Congruence" we have to ensure that they have had the opportunity to interact and build trust, confidence and belief (more of this in a short while in the final chapter dealing with sales today!). Our experience has shown the best ways to do this is by being open and engaging. Ultimately there is a process that salesmen need to go through that enables the buying process to take place. The sales process may be more sequential but it is not rigid. Rigidity or scripting is not advisable as it does not really allow for variance in the responses we may get from customers.

In a recent experience we were delighted when observing a sales person she went off the "track" of the process to answer a customer's pressing question, but skilfully got back to where she needed to be. The important thing to remember is that as salesmen we need certain information in order to match our product and service with customer needs so we do need to have a sales process that addresses that whilst matching a buying process!

For both parties involved in the process of buying and selling there is a lot of personal status at stake. The salesman wants success, the buyer wants honour and respect and if they feel they are being taken for a ride they will soon back away from the purchase. If the buyer is uncertain he will raise an objection which merely means the salesman has not helped him perceive the opportunity represented by the purchase as being greater than the cost in money, time, effort, convenience or whatever else is in the equation. A customer expects to be an equal partner (some perhaps a senior partner!) in the entire process. They want to feel unique and special but not isolated and alone; hence it is reassuring when we deal with objections to use the process we referred to earlier as *feel, felt, found.*

So the balance has to be a buying process, matched by an enabling sales process. When the two ultimately work together they lead to what we consider as "Congruence". This state of "Congruence" is when the salesman and the buyer are agreed on the product or service that is most appropriate for the buyer (customer) and allows them then to move to a state of action in completing the purchase.

Whilst we have noted that the Buying Process is consistent and that all stages must be gone through for it to work successfully, we would also want to be clear that sales processes vary from product to product and probably from organisation to organisation. We have taken snapshots of brand and how sophisticated that now is, incorporating brand personality and values as well as the product and service that represent the brand. It is precisely because of these two issues that competitor sales processes may vary from each other.

We cannot describe a precise sales process here as it does vary and the interpretation of how to use a sales process to match the Buying

Process will obviously vary in line with that. This may well form part of the competitor differentiation in a time when consumerism has also reduced many products and services to a commodity.

Using brand personality and values to drive a sales process which enables a buying process clearly shows difference between one organisation and another. This differentiation can also allow customer choice, even where the product or service has very little difference in and of itself. It is therefore crucial that salesmen representing an organisation carry through those values and exemplify the personality of the organisation. Individuality may be lauded, but within a framework; we do not recommend cloned and personality-less salesmen, but too much individuality can detract from the brand's personality and values.

There are differences in roles, there are differences in techniques but more and more people are perceived as being part of the sales process and there is almost a continuum of sales and service with no break. Organisations that provide business to business links will often engage a broader team in the sales process so that their customers' after sales requirements are understood and managed. This sometimes feels uncomfortable to the salesman who wants to make a sale and finds an accountant saying "We can't do that. Our systems won't allow it". We can only advocate a thorough process of briefing so that "no" or "impossible" are honestly responded to but 'taken away' to be looked at as to do or issues items. Ultimately if it is "no" or "impossible" the customer needs to know, but also we need as an organisation to be able to propose alternatives.

Knowledge here of what competitors can provide and the absolute 'musts' of the client are key and may include some of the elements of "political" awareness discussed earlier in the book. There may be a balance in the decision process of the selling organisation, often at a level more senior than the salesman, whether the investment in turning "no" to "yes" or "impossible" to "possible" is worth while.

We may see that the salesman is partnering his knowledgeable if demanding client and almost championing his case back into the selling organisation. We know that selling is a very emotive and emotional thing and many salesmen identify so closely with their customers it can feel upsetting if they cannot provide what they want. Level heads and negotiation are required here. But all the time we must be aware that a customer is on some kind of journey or undergoing some kind of process that we simply call the buying process. It may be overt or covert, but we have come to realise that it is always present, no matter what we are buying, where or when. Being a customer ourselves is salutary and provides great insight into how we may make better salesmen ourselves!

A Summary

What we have done in the present chapter is to elaborate the most recent and relevant learning that we have brought to bear in the selling environment, which we will explore further shortly.

This is an era of realism because of the economic situation but also one in which the customers are more knowledgeable and have access to more information through the Internet. Almost regardless of what the customer wants to buy they can find information on the web about it...sometimes misleading or incomplete information which may lead to confusion and potential conflict.

Focus in the era

In this section we have used an example of consultancy as our "selling" situation. Very often consumers feel they don't need a consultant and so our Skills have had to heighten.

Motivation and Expectations

Anyone buying in the current environment is looking for value for money from any product or service. The plethora of "comparison" websites indicates a kind of commoditisation as well as the price comparisons. It also indicates the shift in Knowledge and potential "power" in the salesman / customer dynamic. Salesmen have to be much more aware and sensitive.

Brand

With the increased commoditisation marketers have had to make their own products and services stand out from the crowd. Brand covers more that one might first imagine and includes the personality of the product and service. This extends through to the people selling or servicing the product and service. The internal organisational expectations are for conformance by employees.

The Key Elements of Selling

We have found that selling has had to "grow up" and become even more professional to be successful in the present era. There will always be the "distress" or "emergency" purchase but generally with customers being more discerning the interpersonal Behaviours, Attitudes, Skills and Knowledge have had to develop.

Behaviours

The enhancement in Behaviours has been in the areas I elaborate below. Earlier Behaviours remain most significant.

- Networking

In this example but in so many others too, the power of a network was fundamental. Relationship building no matter what one is selling is critical.

- Adapting to modern communication

The more mature salespeople have had to realise that only the traditional methods of communication are insufficient, though talking to someone remains very significant

Attitudes

In addition to the existing Attitudes, salesmen had to be open to the following:

- Customers are more knowledgeable purchasers

Being aware that customers have greater access to Knowledge about products and services and have access to that information is so important.

- Greater Comparison (commoditisation)

It is important to realise that despite our and marketing's best efforts, consumers and the world in general conspires to equate all that we offer.

Skills

This area, along with Knowledge is the one which has changed most dramatically with additions and amendments to the existing Skills

- Handling Objections (feel, felt, found)

With the increase in respect and awareness for individuals it is important to treat their objections more "seriously" too

Knowledge

Building upon existing and new Skills the Knowledge needed to bring it all together and make it appropriate.

The Knowledge included:

- The Buying Process

Probably the single most important insight we have had in the current era is the fact that to sell successfully we need to help a customer through a cycle we refer to as the buying process. Sales processes need to address and enable the buying process.

Reflections

Here we discuss how all the elements come together, how to use them and their significance in being successful.

The Parable of Harry Schmidt

as told by Kieran Maloney

Harry was a master at blending the Skills and Behaviours of a successful salesman. I came across him through and offer made by American Express to buy wine in my own home.

My wife and I were nervous before his arrival, recollecting other attempts by salesmen at our door or in our home. However, this was different; partly because we liked the product but mostly because of Harry himself. What a presence he had and what enthusiasm he was able to generate. He was able to put us at ease instantly and reassured us that the invoice would not be excessive. He had picked up on our anxiety before we had expressed it and stopped a potential objection in its tracks.

The blend of all the Skills, Behaviours and Attitudes is rare to achieve but Harry was a good example of a person who got close to it. Harry's Knowledge was extensive over a range of wines and was born of years of experience in restaurants, hotels and ocean going liners. We probably don't all have that wealth of experience or indeed the need for that breadth of knowledge, but his example is a good one for reminding us of the importance of that most basic of areas of Knowledge, the product we are selling. Harry came to the homes of his clients and helped them explore and discover new wines and extend their palate.

Along the way he matched his Knowledge with our taste and interest. Looking at it now I could say he reached a state of "Congruence" with us as he found what we liked and shared an example of it. The clever thing then was that he moved the parameters slightly to a more robust or a sweeter wine. I never imagined liking sweetish German wines described as Spatlese (late picking) or Auslese (last picking). Nor did I ever realise that I would learn that the longer the grape stayed on the vine the sweeter it would become; Auslese sweeter than a spatlese.

Harry managed the balance of treating customers as king but also addressing their "ignorance" in such a way that they willingly and enthusiastically learned about wines and new tastes. He added good Knowledge to the mix and questioned gently to unravel Attitudes and emotional responses to "new" flavours. By being subtle and extending the repertoire or tastes of individuals a nudge sweeter or drier, or softer or more robust at the ends of the spectrum Harry extended my palate and my enjoyment of a wider range of wines. It can be done!

THE CHALLENGE OF SELLING IN TODAY'S ENVIRONMENT

Let's summarise everything that we have learned from each of the eras and understand how it can be applied to selling in the current era and environment.

We have now arrived at the destination and in doing so hope we have created a semblance of "Congruence" with you - our reader and professional salesman.

In each section we examined Behaviours, Attitudes, Skills and Knowledge (BASK) as they have grown, changed and developed over time and as the demands of being a professional sales person have grown, changed and developed.

It will be of little value to have all of those qualities and capabilities without being able to use them ... like having a great car with no means of starting it perhaps.

The application of those qualities and capabilities will depend on your willingness to embrace and practice them.

From concepts such as ensuring no interruptions to the customer conversation, through understanding the customer's motivation and helping them understand their own real needs, to knowing that the customer is on a journey or undergoing a process too: all are included in applying it all.

Observing people selling, even detaching oneself from the process as a customer, it becomes painfully obvious when inappropriate selling is taking place. Too often we see potential conflicts arise as the salesman pushes product or service. Especially in this era realism we need to work with customers and guide them, enable them, possibly lead them to where they want to go, but pushing is taboo. Coercive selling may exist in certain market places and for certain products, but ethically, morally and respectfully we treat customers as partners on the journey. Our sales process needs to be aligned to the customers buying process. Push and they will resist; guide, lead, encourage and listen and they may well follow.

It is not for us here to make moral, ethical or social judgements but our experience is that customers expect to be treated respectfully and will stubbornly refuse to buy if we try to lead them where they are unwilling to follow. So even if we do not push, we need to be careful in our approach.

Often we notice that the so-called "pushy" salesman has not paid attention to the buying process and has probably assumed 'willingness' in their customer. We need to ensure for each sale that we have allowed a customer to travel the journey of the buying process, no matter how quick it may be, it is necessary.

Recently we have experienced what may be called the "two-pronged" cold call. One cheery soul starts off to engage with you as a potential client and starts to explore with leading, rather than open questions what you might do "if...". He then tells you to "hang on" and hands over to a new voice which comes in, "Hi, I understand you....."

The second voice may not assume willingness, but is probably assuming trust or confidence or belief and is making no attempt to build them. So as a customer we may feel that we have been softened up by the first voice with which we had not got beyond an interaction stage; then along comes Jolly Voice Two assuming trust and we have none. It must work on some people or it would not exist, however we would say that is likely to be far less successful than if we build a true communication with the customer.

Inappropriate sales can occur in many ways; assuming stages on the customer's buying process, leading customers and making assumptions about their needs, wants or desires before they have expressed them or in general being "pushy" in trying to get the sale rather than enabling the customer to buy!

Whereas in earlier times we may have seen impulsive buying or examples of "I'll have it because I can", in the era of reality, knowledgeable and cautious customers are much more circumspect. This seems to be having an effect upon salesmen: at one extreme salesmen may appear to have capitulated ("they will buy if they are going to buy") or at the other extreme a steely determination that customers will buy from me ("I'll make them buy from me ...I'll convince them"). The former is not necessary as there are still people with money and dependent upon what the product or service there is still a need to buy. The latter shows some of the character and determination of the salesman but ignores that the customers and the world in general is more cautious but equally more demanding. There is almost an unwritten or unspoken law from the customer that says "I am the customer: respect me and treat me as if I am intelligent. I'll have none of your nonsense".

Personal bias or predispositions can come to play. Salesmen need to be aware of their own prejudices and guard against them. Often these may be wrongly based upon age, assuming youngsters are inexperienced and will buy anything or assuming older people are confused and don't know what is what! The cautionary words are, make no assumptions.

Many sales situations may not be resolved in one meeting and some will require the involvement of more than one person from the sales organisation. We need also to consider that the buyer may be more than one person, even in a domestic situation where partners increasingly will share key decisions. This calls for consistency in so many ways.

Consistency may most easily be achieved with factual information, but even here it can go awry if basic facts and customer requirements are not established. Prices and specifications may change even in a short space of time but trust, confidence and belief can be destroyed if we just talk to an existing potential customer as if they know about changes. For example someone buying a new house on a "new build site" may be interested in a particular property on paper and have shown that interest to the sales team. Imagine the price has been reduced by a certain amount and the specification of the kitchen fitments has changed. Consistency in this inconsistent state can be achieved only if we have kept a good record of the potential clients, when and where they stated their interested and a sensitive explanation of the changes, acknowledging they are changes.

Consistency between individuals involved in a sale must exist if we are to maintain trust, confidence and belief. Fred says X and James says Y is a recipe for confusing a customer and leading them away from the selling organisation. At an organisational level these potential hiccoughs need to be addressed by good record keeping, good communication and good training. Individuals can also address this issue by ensuring they communicate, record, respect colleagues and follow processes set down within an organisation.

We have seen examples of organisational inconsistency whereby a team of sales people were trying to persuade existing customers onto new products and services while a neighbouring retention team was trying to keep existing customers on the same product or service. Inconsistency can happen at so many levels and in several ways. Every individual has a responsibility to maintain consistency for and with a customer.

Perhaps another aspect of consistency is a consistent view of the customer. Think back to the example of selling furniture to the corporate buyer and the complexity of who was the true customer. Think more simply of the domestic situation where one partner has shown initial interest and the other will be very much involved and influential in the decision making processes. In an organisation it may be seen as a "decision making unit" but we should not ignore the fact that they may well exist in a domestic situation. Who selects the family holiday perhaps?

What sometimes militates against that is that the salesman "imposes" his own situation and beliefs in how it will be. This is another form of assumption whereby as salesmen we run the danger of assuming others do things the same way as we do, or have the same budgets or beliefs and values as us. We could simply repeat the warning of "don't assume" but perhaps we should add, "Find out instead".

The customer or client is not ourselves and all that has gone before has been designed to help us establish who the customer is and what their needs are. We have found salesmen who have been averse to finding out the whole set of requirements and needs of the customer. This may well be because the specification of what we have to sell does not fit within or match exactly those requirements. It is a question then of establishing priorities and what are the "unbreakable" requirements. It is ultimately the customer's choice so why not find out what they want and then do our best to match those requirements?

The importance of establishing customer or client needs is fundamental in matching but also in helping the customer through the buying process. The integrated approach of ensuring that open, not leading questions are asked, that we listen, that we respond and that we enable the customer to feel respected and as if they are a valued partner in this decision is critical to success.

What makes our customers demand this type of equality may well stem from the fact that they are well informed about both our, and our competitor products and services. As we have said, sometimes the information they have may not be accurate and, sadly some of it is designed to confuse or mislead. It is our responsibility as salesmen to ensure that customers understand completely and are in a situation to compare apples with apples.

This process requires sensitivity as we do not want our customer to feel that they are wrong. Thus we need to guide them carefully and explain without making them feel that it is their "fault" they have the misguided view. Nor should we belittle our competitors but merely be factual and this requires that our own knowledge of products and competitor offerings have to be up to date and true.

There is also an implication strategically that the information on our own websites is accurate and up to date and that the information we have as salesmen is consistent with the website. This coordination and consistency is hugely important for organisational credibility. Consider the impact upon the customer's trust, confidence and belief if the information on the web is inconsistent with what we as salesmen are saying!

We are seeing changes in customer attitudes as the era changes to greater and greater reality and increases in knowledge are prevalent. Whilst there are many motivational and driving attitudes that we as salesmen need to maintain and which are consistent with attitudes from earlier eras, we need to increase our attitudinal awareness of the customer.

One area that we have deliberately omitted was the attitude of superiority. It was never really a great asset to a salesman, although the self-confidence it encouraged, when appropriately displayed, may be well founded. What is critical in the era of knowledge and realism is an attitude of equality and partnership or sharing. That the salesman once had the knowledge which put him in a position of power is less and less acceptable in these days of equality.

Attitudes do change, or at least some do, and we need to be aware of those. We also need to be sensitive to the fact that not everyone's behaviour and attitudes are the same. Individuality is important too although we all like to belong or feel part of something collectively. This can work for or against a salesman who may see themselves and their organisation as the in-group and everyone outside the organisation as an out group and therefore either not so well informed or, worse still as an "inferior" being. Yes, we have seen that happen and we know that the attitude of superiority does not work in these days. The old maxim of pride comes before a fall is still very true if that pride is misplaced.

So we need to be "on equal terms" with our clients to be successful. Yes we can be the knowledge expert but nonetheless we need to be sensitive to the fact that we are not superior. Empathy is probably an over used and misunderstood term. What we mean by it here is an ability to understand our customer, their situation, their need and wants and to be able to recommend solutions to those needs which are appropriate.

Selling is about providing answers to a client or customer's needs and wants in line with their ability to pay for what's on offer. I need transport, for example and I desire a Rolls Royce but in reality I can only afford a Ford Focus. Empathy will understand all of this and offer an appropriate solution that meets my needs and as far as possible addresses my emotional state. What alternatives can be offered that help resolve the debate the customer has within himself? Is it a brand new but more basic model or a pre-owned vehicle that is of a higher specification? Ultimately it is the customer's choice, but if we can empathise and offer suitable, carefully thought out alternatives we are respecting the customer's true needs. Remember true needs are often based upon our emotional rather than our logical needs.

"Congruence" – Successful Selling

Underpinning all the sales techniques, the Attitudes, the Skills, the Knowledge, the Behaviours of the professional sales person is the ability to present the proposition of their organisation to a prospective buyer in a way that will ensure a successful outcome for the customer, the company and the sales person.

This can only be consistently achieved when that sales presentation, in whatever format, is aligned to the Buying Process that every customer undertakes every time they make a purchase.

By understanding this Buying Process it is possible for the professional sales person to customise their sales presentation to align with that Buying Process and in doing so ensure that the customer, their organisation and they themselves reach a point of "Congruence".

Before analysing and understanding the Buying Process it is important to become aware of the probable motivators that might have influenced the potential purchaser. The influencing effect of brand, advertising, recommendation, reputation, publicity or previous experience can not only motivate the potential purchaser but may establish expectations that, if they are not fulfilled during the Buying Process, will adversely affect the buying decision.

In this era influencing is probably increasing as knowledge is more easily shared and found. It is also germane to recognise that social networks, where people are sharing personal experience. Likes and dislikes, are influencing an unknown range of people.

It is therefore incumbent on the sales person to ensure that, in their dealings with the potential purchaser or client they demonstrate the values of the organisation they represent and enhance the proposition offered.

"Congruence" is represented as a triangle because there is always a larger number of prospective purchasers that enter the process than ultimately become actual purchasers. Every individual who makes a purchase HAS to go through this buying process; from the individual simply buying a loaf of bread in the local store to the company buyer signing a purchase order for the supply of fleet vehicles.

The only flexibility in the Buying Process is the time line each purchase takes.

"Congruence" in Action

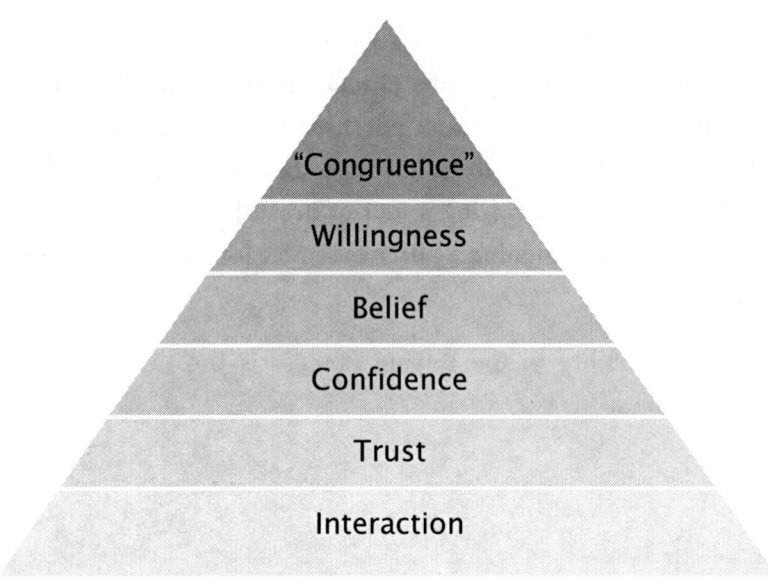

This process happens no matter what we buy. Sometimes, especially on regular and repeat purchases the stages may be accelerated and possibly more subliminal than when it is a new or unique purchase. There is no real timescale attached to the process and, although there is logic to the order, it is possible that we can disturb a stage and have to revisit it and it is possible that we may accelerate one stage into the next. It is really dependent, as a buyer, upon the efforts of the salesperson.

Interaction

The Buying Process starts with an interaction between the potential purchaser and the organisation that hopes to sell the potential product or service. The interaction could be entering a shop, picking up the telephone, responding on a web site, e-mailing or approaching a market stall and communicating by word or deed with the potential seller or selling organisation.

The interaction stage can have several forms but it is the first real communication between the selling organisation and the buyer *for the purchase in question.* I italicise the last few words as it is often the case that a customer is returning for a repeat purchase. The interesting thing is that the customer will go through the same process each time. Yes, the more frequent and familiar the purchase the more one may say that the preliminary stages are speeded up or made less obvious; they are nonetheless there and important.

The interaction, as we said, may take several forms; dropping by to a retail outlet, using a "contact us" page on the web, calling to a contact centre, responding to an advertisement or inviting a representative to visit our home. Usually the customer is pro-active but sometimes the initial interaction results from a "cold call", promotional leaflet, a representative making neighbourhood visits or some form of presence in a High Street encouraging and educating people about our service or product.

Whatever prompts the contact, it is that contact we refer to as an interaction. How the potential seller may respond to that interaction will vary according to what is being sold, the existing relationship with the customer or the environment in which the interaction takes place. Someone buying a sandwich at the local shop will expect, and probably receive different interaction from one who is beginning and enquiry about, say a new car. The range of approaches and responses is endless and, like the types of open questions we may ask, cause us to run out of space here if we listed all of them. Even if we did we could well miss a specific example!

We have expressed our slightly jaundiced view of what is referred to as rapport. We believe that true rapport takes a very long time to establish. However, the alignment of the sales process, which by its nature must be flexible, with the Buying Process which is rigid creates a reaction in both parties which has the potential for developing an appropriate relationship.

In short the *Interaction* is the platform on which the sale will be made. How the potential purchaser is treated at this stage is critical. They will have entered this stage with some expectations – if these expectations are met or exceeded then they will start to move to the next stage, if not they may well withdraw at this stage.

Herewith is a word of caution. To ensure a successful sale the potential purchaser has to go through every stage of the process. The over enthusiastic sales person who pre-empts the decision to buy will lose the sale.

Trust

Although we describe the process sequentially it is important to remember that we can be working at several levels at once and one error can send the whole process tumbling like a house of cards. Conversely, getting it right can help accelerate through the overall process and enhance later stages or reaffirm earlier stages.

By trust here we mean several things: they are to do with the trustworthiness of the salesman, the product, the service and the organisation. Also there is the beginning of a notion of trust that the product or service will meet my requirements. The old adage of "people buy from people" may well be at its truest here. On yet another level trust is the feeling engendered when the expectations of the potential purchaser are met or exceeded. In this case it confirms the potential purchaser's decision to interact with this organisation appear to be vindicated.

Trust is very much an emotional response, supported by the logical thought process, but primarily emotional. Subconsciously the customer is thinking "Do I like this person?" "Do I like what is happening here?" "Does this feel like a place / organisation I can do business with?"

Apocryphal stories exist of the individual who goes to a "posh" or up-market car show room wearing jeans and appearing unkempt. The salesman supposedly does not feel the customer has the wherewithal to afford such a car and treats him disdainfully. So the guy walks away and buys elsewhere. The story has it that he is a multi-millionaire and could easily afford the upmarket product. His trust in the salesman and the organisation do not exist from an emotional response that starts from a disliking of the way he is being treated more than of the person per se.

Returning to the idea of "people buy from people", it is important to realise that to the customer the person selling to them, or interacting with them *is* the organisation. So trust in the organisation can be hugely impacted by the responses of the individual. Fortunately for organisations they are able to build a reputation that is bigger than an individual transaction or response, but they do need to be aware of the impact, especially on a first time customer, of their employees and representatives.

How we build trust is a hugely individual thing and again has dependency upon the circumstances, the situation, the customer and the product or service we are selling. Appropriateness is the by-word again and the building of trust has to be genuine and we have to be aware of how fragile it can be, especially in the early stages and how damaged it can be at any time.

For a complex sale or high value or life changing product trust becomes more and more significant. But consider the damage that can be made to trust if my regular shopping reveals something substandard or unpleasant; or if the shop I regularly use has an assistant who treats me wrongly? Trust, for any of us as a customer is crucial and may play an even stronger part in my purchase decision with one off purchases especially where the emotional content of the decision is high.

Confidence

If we feel trusting and sense honesty, sincerity and genuine consideration coming from the salesperson, as a customer we can start to feel more confident. We should consider once again that confidence is built on multi-levels: in the salesman, in the product or service and in the organisation. The customer will be considering his level of confidence in each of those respective areas. But confidence has to be "about" something. So the musings will be "How confident am I that this person can deliver what he is talking about? How confident am I that this product and service really will do what I want and need? How confident am I that this organisation will deliver, support and make this process as hassle free as possible?"

Building the required level of confidence may not be easy but it will be easy to lose it or shatter it by not treating the customer correctly. Yet again we have to say that building confidence is unique in each set of circumstances and each organisation needs to consider how it will build and maintain consumer confidence.

Again confidence is largely built upon emotion and interpersonal connectivity and only supported by logic and knowledge. It is possible to restore confidence and evidence shows that a dissatisfied customer who has his complaint dealt with effectively may be more loyal than one who has no complaint at all. However, if we are trying to sell to them in the first instance we have to ensure their confidence and trust are there and well established, and we should not consider that there is a back-stop of customer services if we get it wrong. Although this may produce a loyal customer, it is also costly to an organisation to rectify errors. The old maxim of "get it right first time" is not a bad one!

We must say that most people get parts of it right and the general British customer can be quite forgiving. We also do not want to create the image that a salesman has to be some kind of super hero in order to get it right. However we do need to draw a distinction between a successful salesman and those that get by. A successful salesman will add these ideas to his awareness and blend them into his mix of delivery. What we can honestly say is that those who understand and make attempts to adopt this notion of a buying process change their success profile quite dramatically. We are not advocating that every salesman needs to be a sensitive being; what we are advocating is that to be successful it certainly helps to be aware of the impact of what we do upon a customer and potential customer.

Bear in mind that facts, especially to those people who live their lives in the factual and analytical zone, play an important part in building trust and confidence. As a customer my response may be more from my emotional than logical side but trust and confidence may well stem from somebody who knows what they are talking about. A similar response may be exemplified away from selling. I am more likely to trust and have confidence in a doctor who tells me what can be done and how as well as alerting me to side effects than one who promises me "everything will be alright".

Underpinning confidence is consistency. In this age of knowledgeable and informed prospects the sales person must be consistent with the brand image and provide information that is totally aligned to the advertising, P.R and proposition of the company for whom they are selling.

I hope that you are beginning to see the link between understanding your customer and the process you need to adopt to deliver to them as an individual. This is where the blend of the art and science side of selling comes in. The art is weaving the tools and awareness to meet an individual and the science is knowing there is a structure or framework, but not sticking rigidly to a formulaic approach.

Belief

This is one of the most crucial stages in the buying process and as salesmen we ignore it at our peril. Thinking of yourself as a customer of this methodology we are outlining, you may well have cottoned on to, and seen value in, open questions. By listening to the customer and understanding them as individuals we may have, even through these pages, built trust and confidence on the platform of interaction you created by reading this book. There may remain though that element of doubt because you have been successful until now so why adopt these ideas even though they are born of experience and some understanding of people. The more we push the more you may resist....and yes we have learned from experience and so we do not push. We understand that you may feel doubtful; several others that we have worked with have felt exactly the same way. All we can say is that those who have built a sales process that they have aligned to the buying process have found that they improved their success.

Let's be honest we do not believe everything all the time. In writing this the word processor software throws up our errors in spelling and grammar. Generally we believe that they are right but sometimes our experience or a need to say something in a particular way tells us not to believe what we see. We make a judgement in the same way that customers are judging their belief in salesman, product, service or organisation. Their questions now might be "Do I believe this is right for me? Do I believe it will do what it says on the tin?"

This is a critical stage that has to be built upon trust and confidence and is often the area from which "objections" arise. Patience, listening, rebuilding and understanding true needs, helping a customer to see that the opportunity is greater than the cost are all and each an important contributor to the ultimate belief.

Some belief is "blind" in that we just expect it. Many individuals have bought a car without looking under the bonnet or understanding the specification of tyres, brakes or suspension and gear ratios. Instead they respond to leather seating, surround sound and heated seating. The fact that the car has an engine, will start and operate safely and successfully are taken for granted. That is blind belief if you will.

Belief then can be based upon logic, it can be based upon emotion or it can be based upon a combination of both. It is, though, probably one of the most critical factors in people's purchase intentions.

To help our customer to recognise, acknowledge and understand their own belief we use open questions – What are you looking for in a car? What would that mean to you? How would your family feel in a new car?

The questions are endless – but delivered with genuine interest in the answers they will develop belief as long as the trust and confidence are well established.

Willingness

Only when the prospective customer has trust, confidence and belief in the product, proposition, sales person and organisation will they become willing to take the next step and make the ultimate purchase.

So how does this stage of willingness arise?

It will only emerge when all of the stages have been successfully navigated, all the questions have been answered honestly and effectively the customer has communicated their belief in the proposition and you, the sales professional, have asked for the business. Even small and seemingly insignificant purchases require the same effort.

We can never take willingness for granted. There is no harm in trialling a close to test willingness and "outing" objections. Very often in our experience salespeople have been too timid to do that. Sometimes we need to test willingness, but we should never assume it.

"Congruence"

"Congruence" is a state of agreement and harmony.

Our search has been a Journey to "Congruence". Perhaps we have arrived at the destination so what is it? There is an action element on the part of the customer that probably speaks for itself in that it means the customer taking action, which will usually mean making a purchase or creating a purchase order.

At this stage the sales professional should recognise why this stage of "Congruence" exists and be alert to any threats to the agreement and harmony that exists.

A simple example of this is when the door of the office in which you have conducted the successful sales presentation opens. A colleague of your newly acquired customer comes in and asks what the customer has been buying! This is a potential threat to "Congruence".

Let us just introduce another concept. In many complex sales situations it is possible that the 'sale' is of a proposition that the 'purchaser' has to 'buy' before it is presented to a committee or senior manager. The "Congruence" in this case will mean obtaining a favourable decision to take the purchase to the next step.

We first realised the significance of this in the buying process when working with a particular client whose sale was staged over three events. The second, middle step, involved a qualified expert, who was not a sales person, using their expertise to identify and recommend a particular course of action to the potential customer. By encouraging the expert to explain the rationale of their recommendation to the potential customer and gaining agreement from the customer that the recommendation matched their requirements we were able to help the expert and the potential customer reach a state of 'harmony and agreement' – "Congruence"

The expert now passed the potential customer to the sales person who then went into their sales presentation. They started at Interaction and built trust and confidence as a platform to belief which led to willingness and finally to "Congruence"

An important reminder – a new interaction means that the customer will be going through the Buying Process again. We must never make the assumption they are ready to buy – they may be but they may not! Do not waste all your hard work because you assume.

 "Congruence" is the state where objections have been overcome, the client is willing to purchase and both the client and the salesman have agreed all the relevant details. Depending upon the type of product or service "Congruence" may be arrived at very quickly or it may take many months.

The Buying Process will always be the purchaser's route to a decision however long that decision takes.

In Conclusion

Whether this is a "happily ever after" story or not is down to how well we embrace the needs of the customer in how we sell to them. Whether you buy our concepts or not will be dependent upon how well we have helped you to understand our message. You may believe part of it will work but not all of it.

We have been through eras spanning over forty years in which the process of selling has changed although there have been many constants. The contexts of the eras, the amount people have had to spend, the freedom they have had to spend and the access of information have been large parts of what has driven change.

Success to a salesman has consistently been recognised as closing a sale or many sales but how that success is achieved has changed over time. We have described four elements in the delivery or perhaps in the "make up" of the salesman. Those elements are Behaviours, Attitudes, Skills and Knowledge shortened by the acronym BASK. We have included the key elements of BASK from each era that have carried forward and remain important today. Some have emerged or developed as time has moved on, mostly Skills or Knowledge, and some have evolved without radically changing, Behaviours and Attitudes. It is possibly true that Attitudes change as we grow older but they also change with the values of the society of which we are part.

Rather than *selling to* people, we are more inclined to enable people to *buy from* us. This requires new Skills and Knowledge but also reflects a change in Attitude, believing that the customer is a partner and so on. This Attitude is probably the new norm for people entering the field of sales now but for those who have been in sales for a while the change may be difficult. Many of us do not notice change as it can be so gradual, then all of a sudden we realise that change has taken place and we need to shift too. As the seasons change we may not see every change day by day but suddenly trees are in leaf or denuded of their leaves. Similarly with the changes in selling, we may not notice the subtle changes that take place as a new era establishes it self until the whole perspective looks different.

As yet we do not know what they are, but a new era will emerge and with it new perspectives of customers and salespeople. Probably it will continue the shift of "power" from the salesman to the customer; it seems unlikely that it will go backwards. Will a new era emerge where customers have greater freedom to buy and the shackles of economic concern disappear? We cannot predict but we do know the process will be gradual and that most of what we have talked about here will remain relevant.

In conclusion we will remind you of the totality of Behaviours, Attitudes, Skills and Knowledge that have accumulated to bring about the success of the salesman in this era of realism. Good luck and good selling.

In search of Congruence

ERA	Consolidation	Expansion	Ambition	Reality
Key Elements	BASK	BASK +	BASK ++	BASK +++
Control and lead	Salesman in control	Salesman in control	Salesman and buyer share control (on par)	Buyer in control
Personality	Personality selling	Presentation or more formal	Relationship, presentation and expertise	Mirror the buying process
The Representation	Salesman represents the company	Salesman represents the style	Salesman represents the Consistency	Salesman represents the Brand
Understanding	A personal view (know the type of the buyer)	Know the group	People, expertise, open questions and handle objection	CONGRUENCE

Summary of BASK

Behaviours

In the era of consolidation

- Preparation

- Awareness

- Respectfulness

- Time "management"

- Reliability

- Recording

- Reporting

Additions and changes in the era of expansion

- Perseverance

- Patience

- Consistency

Additions in the era of ambition

- Increased customer awareness

- Availability to customers

Final additions in the era of reality

- Customer awareness

- Networking

- Adapting to modern communication methods and styles

- Use of the web

Attitudes

In the era of Consolidation

- Positivity

- Focus

- Winning

- Competitive

- Strong

- Realistic

- Ambitious

- Divine Discontent

Additions in the era of expansion, ambition

- Is the customer King?

- Attitudes are generally consistent but may need greater attention or focus along with the changing "sales climate"

Additions in the era of reality

- Consumer awareness

- Customer as Knowledgeable purchaser

- Greater Comparison (commoditisation)

Skills

In the era of consolidation

- Interpersonal (Social, Communication, Engagement)
- Control
- Questioning and Listening
- Presentation
- Objection Handling
- Closing (including creating Buying Mood)
- Positioning

Additions in the era of expansion

- Empathy
- Negotiation

Additions or changes in the era of ambition

- Personality and Behaviour identification
- Open Questions
- Creating the Opportunity to be bigger than the cost
- Presenting to needs and wants
- Handling objections

Additions or changes in the era of reality

- Heightened interpersonal

- Handling objections (feel, felt, found)

- Treating Customers as Knowledgeable partners

- Use of Multi Media

- Appropriate Communication using new Media

Knowledge

In the era of consolidation

- Product Knowledge

- Competitors Products

- Market Knowledge

Additions in the era of expansion

- Political awareness

- Political levers

Additions in the era of ambition

- Personality style and Behaviour cues

- Open Questions

- A developed network

Additions in the era of reality

- Sales to service continuum

- The buying process and "Congruence"

Lightning Source UK Ltd.
Milton Keynes UK
UKOW030629210812

197832UK00006B/1/P